BECAUSE NO ONE IS GOING TO TAKE CARE OF YOU

A Guide to Financial Success for the Recent Graduate

Second Edition

C. MICHAEL SMITH

ISBN-13: 978-0-9904782-2-5

CONTENTS

Disclaimer   i

Foreword   iii

Prologue   vii

PART I – GETTING STARTED & MAKING MONEY

1. Starting a Career   1
2. The Entrepreneurial Option   13
3. Get a Handle on Your Current Situation   23

PART II – SAVINGS, TAXES & INSURANCE

4. Banking & Saving   39
5. Maintaining a Rainy-Day Fund   53
6. An Overview of Taxes   61
7. Risk Protection   73

PART III – GOING INTO & COMING OUT OF DEBT

8. Using a Credit Card Responsibly   85
9. Paying-for & Paying-off a Higher Education   97
10. Autos & Housing   107

PART IV – INVESTING FOR YOUR FUTURE

11. Investing Basics   117
12. Using Retirement Plans   139
13. Choosing a Financial Advisor   151

Epilogue   161

End Notes   168

Glossary   169

DISCLAIMER

This book is provided for general information only. You should not treat any opinion expressed by the author as a specific inducement to make a particular investment or follow a particular strategy. You must make an independent decision regarding the investments and strategies mentioned in this book. This book is not comprehensive and may not cover all financial strategies that are pertinent to you. When investing, past performance is not indicative of future results. You should be aware of the real risk of loss in following any investment strategy and the fact that you may get back less than you invested. Before acting on information in this book, you should consider whether it is suitable for your particular circumstances and strongly consider seeking advice from your own financial or investment adviser.

◆ FOREWORD ◆

"I wish I had this book thirty years ago."

That's the thought that kept echoing in my head as I read the first edition of Mike's book, *Because No One is Going to Take Care of You*. If you are like me and are starting to look at winding down your career rather than beginning it, you are going to wish you had this book when you were younger. I wish I could go back and force my younger self to implement the advice that Mike has provided here. But this book isn't for me – it is for the "recent" graduate who, unlike me, has time. As Mike points out in his book – "time" is your best ally when it comes to financial planning. If you are a member of our younger generations, then you have time, and I sincerely hope that you read this book and heed its advice.

While I didn't have this great resource in my twenties, I was lucky in that I actually got to know Mike (now Dr. Smith) in my thirties. Even long before these books were written, Mike was an authority on all things investing and finance. He was the first person to ever speak to me about "financial planning". Thanks to his sound financial wisdom (and willingness to share it with me), I was able to get my financial life in order in my thirties and begin to move forward in life with an increased ability to make good decisions regarding my future and retirement planning. I was very fortunate! You are even more fortunate in that you can get started even earlier than I did – and that can make a huge difference for you.

Knowing Mike for all these years, I can say that reading *Because No One is Going to Take Care of You* is like sitting down and having a conversation with him. No reader will feel like they are reading a personal finance textbook. You will feel like you are having a discussion with a friend who really cares about your financial success – you will feel a sense of empowerment in your ability to get a hold of your financial future. Mike goes through everything you need – step-by-step while pointing out pitfalls and different ways to succeed. He also provides many unbiased resources to guide you along the way. He knows that what might work for some people may not work for others. Therefore, he starts you down the good path and gives you the knowledge and the resources you need to continue the journey in a way that is tailored to your needs. All of this support and advice is done with wit, humor, and a straightforwardness that no other finance writer (I know of) is able to approach.

As the Principal of Washington-Lee High School in Arlington, Virginia, I have been introduced to hundreds of young people – many of whom I am able to stay in contact with for years after graduation. Some of them find jobs after they graduate high school, but many more go on to college. Interestingly, I have found that it doesn't matter whether they go to school or go to work – when asked, most of them state that they struggle with their personal finances. All of them need financial advice and many of them have no idea where to go to find it—at least not without having to pay out a significant amount of money! Whenever possible, I give them a copy of Mike's book, or at the very least, recommend they get it. This book is, quite honestly, the best financial advice I can give to my younger friends. In fact, by the time you read this, I will have given copies of this second edition to my own son, niece and nephews since I know this will help them get a head start on their financial success as they continue their journey into adulthood.

Like Mike, I worry about the financial futures of today's young people. I'm comforted to know that Mike continues to teach his students these concepts in his classes and in his writing. This is his passion – let him help you. With this informative and thought-provoking book, you can be on your way to a more financially successful future! I am very proud to say I took his advice, just as you should do today.

Gregg Robertson, Ed.D.
Principal, Washington-Lee High School

♦ PROLOGUE ♦

NO ONE IS GOING TO TAKE CARE OF YOU

Are your parents rich – I mean really, really rich? The kind of "rich" so that you have no choice but to be rich too? If so, then that is great news! But while you are welcome to read on, this book may not be for you. This book is for the recent graduate (from high school or college) who is not expecting a big inheritance. This book is for those graduates who are heading out into the workforce and find themselves on their own for the first time. Is this you?

Perhaps you have student loans and a sense of unease about paying them off. Perhaps you are looking for a job in your area of interest but haven't had much luck. Or perhaps you have already landed a job, and know you should be saving for the future, but you just never seem to have any money left over to invest... Perhaps you are worried that you are making poor financial choices, but just don't know the right things to be doing. Is this you?

If so, then this book is for you. Over the next few hours as you read, I am going to try to convey several things. First off – I'm going to make you feel worse. Yes... if you don't start making smart financial choices, the situation is probably worse than you think. Your generation has a lot working against you, and because of this, your financial future is in significant jeopardy.

But I'm not going to depress you further and leave you to sulk in your own misery with no hope. In fact, there is a lot you can do! After you finish this opening segment (which is the further depressing part of the book), we are going to discuss how you can make those smart financial choices. As you continue to read, you will receive insights into many of the financial choices that you may currently be facing. In everyday terms, you will learn what you can do to improve your chances of having financial success in life.

Act! - Knowing is only half the battle

Before becoming a personal finance lecturer and writer, I worked as a financial advisor. In essence, people would pay me a fee to give them financial advice. During this time, I learned a lot about finances, but I learned even more about human nature. One fact about my time as a financial advisor, that you may find surprising, is that a great number of people are not as well off as they seem to be. Many of my clients were living far above their means and enjoying lifestyles that they could not afford over the long haul (more about this aspect of human nature in chapter eight). Another potentially surprising fact is that while the majority of my clients were interested to learn what they needed to do to get their financial lives in order, most never actually implemented the advice. More often than not, they would fail to take the steps they knew they needed to take to be financially successful because they just couldn't make the sacrifice. One of the saddest lessons I have learned about human nature is that *many people will refuse to make small sacrifices now even if they are certain there will be dire consequences later*.

Perhaps I wasn't a very good financial advisor. It's possible that I needed to be more forthright regarding the importance of acting on the advice. Given this history, I don't want to make the same mistake with you; so please allow me to be blunt! It is simply not good enough to just "know" the right things! As you read this book, you must act on the recommendations that are pertinent to you if you want to have a chance of being financially successful. Knowing the right thing is not enough – you must DO the right thing. Students and recent graduates frequently tell me that they plan to make the necessary changes in their personal finances… They have great intentions! I'm sure you also have great intentions, but with no follow-through, you'd be surprised how quickly you will become your parents' age and still "planning" to make a positive change. Acting right now – today – is the only way to be successful. Procrastination is your worst enemy when it comes to making smart financial choices. Let me give you an example:

I have a friend named Bob who is 66 years old. After he graduated college at age 22, he didn't feel like he was able to save any money. He didn't start saving until he was 32 years old, but at age 32, he was diligent about saving $2,000 per year for the next 35 years (for a total of $70,000 worth of savings). Bob earned an average return of 9% on his savings and at age 66; his $2,000 per year (or $70,000 total) had grown to $470,249. Not too bad…

but this wasn't enough for poor Bob to retire. He is still working.

My friend Sue is also 66 years old. After graduation at age 22, she saved $2,000 a year for 10 years for a total of only $20,000 and then she quit saving. Notice that she has actually "saved" $50,000 less than Bob. She hasn't saved anything for 35 years, but her $20,000 has been earning 9% every year just like Bob's. Do you think she is worse off or better off than Bob?

Sue's account is actually worth $676,123! She has over $200,000 more than Bob! How is it that she is better off? She didn't procrastinate. See Exhibit P-1 on the next page for more information.

If this example isn't enough to motivate you to act today, let's talk about how things are actually worse than you think. Today, many retirees who have not made financially smart decisions throughout their lives are somewhat spared from a lifetime of bad decision-making. As U.S. workers reach a certain age, they qualify for monthly payments from the federal government. These payments, known as Social Security benefits, have helped millions of people to have some income in retirement. Sounds great right? But here is the thing – I don't really think you are going to receive anything close to the amounts that current retirees are receiving. You will receive much, much less… Let me walk you through my logic

Dependence – Independence - Dependence

In the book, "The 7 Habits of Highly Successful People", author Stephen Covey discusses a concept known as "The Maturity Continuum". This concept discusses how the seven habits of successful people work together to take people from "dependence" to "independence" and finally to "interdependence".

EXHIBIT P-1

	The Impact of Procrastination			
	Savings Earning 9% Annually			
Age	Bob's Savings	Bob's Account	Sue's Savings	Sue's Account
22	-	-	2,000	2,180
23	-	-	2,000	4,556
24	-	-	2,000	7,146
25	-	-	2,000	9,969
26	-	-	2,000	13,047
27	-	-	2,000	16,401
28	-	-	2,000	20,057
29	-	-	2,000	24,042
30	-	-	2,000	28,386
31	-	-	2,000	33,121
32	2,000	2,180	-	36,101
33	2,000	4,556	-	39,351
34	2,000	7,146	-	42,892
35	2,000	9,969	-	46,752
45	2,000	56,722	-	110,680
55	2,000	167,402	-	262,020
65	2,000	429,422	-	620,296
66	2,000	$470,249	-	$676,123

To briefly paraphrase Dr. Covey, when we are dependent, we are counting on others to take care of us. When you were a child, you had absolutely no way to support yourself on your own. All of us are dependent on others at the beginning of our lives. But most of us mature. We find that we don't like being dependent on others, so we strive for independence, or the ability to take care of ourselves. Many recent graduates are moving from dependence to independence for the first time. It can be scary but if you find yourself here; you are doing the right thing. You are moving toward success!

Covey then discusses "interdependence" where some truly successful people are able to further mature. In this stage, we are able to work with others to achieve things that none of us would be able to do on our own. I love this concept and actually teach from this book in some of my leadership classes. However, these, are the habits of "successful" people. A growing number of people are not "successful". A much less successful (but arguably more popular) trend might look more like: dependence – independence – and then back to dependence. Let's discuss for a moment – the baby boomers.

After World War II ended, many American troops returned home after years of being away. They were naturally very happy to be reunited with their families. In fact, because of this long-awaited reunion, there was a huge jump in birth rates during this time period. Approximately 76 million "baby boomers" (as this group is known) were born between 1946 and 1964. If you do the math, you can figure out that the baby boomers have just started hitting traditional retirement ages – and there are a bunch of them!

The baby boomers are a fun group, but on the whole, they have not been particularly known for careful long-term financial planning. This isn't to say that all baby boomers have not saved successfully. I know many baby boomers who have done a fantastic job – but many more have not. So, how will they retire? They are going to need your help.

Social Security

The baby boomers are heavily dependent on Social Security to help fund their retirements. They need it! They also feel entitled to it. Social programs like Social Security are sometimes referred to as "entitlement" programs because recipients feel "entitled" to receive their benefits. And why shouldn't they? The working baby boomers have paid taxes all their work-lives to help fund Social Security. The Social Security fund doesn't just magically appear. If you work (legally); you pay into it (we will talk more about this in chapter six). The logic is: As you work – you pay into Social Security – as you retire – you receive payments from Social Security.

But here is the problem: the fund isn't large enough. As I stated before, the baby boomers are a very large group of people. With advancements in health care, they are also likely to live (and continue to withdraw Social Security payments) a very long time. I'm oversimplifying things a little here, but in essence, what we have is a fund that has much more coming out of it than going into it. This will continue to deplete the fund until there is perhaps nothing left.

We know this is a problem. Michele Wucker (in a wonderful book of the same name) would likely refer to this problem as a "Gray Rhino" – a highly probable, high impact yet neglected threat. The warning signs are there, but it is just too easy to do nothing. Unfortunately, politicians avoid addressing Social Security like the plague. Since the baby boomers are such a large group, they carry a lot of political power. They vote! And they don't want Social Security touched. President George W. Bush (bravely or stupidly – depending on your political affiliation) decided to take on the Social Security problem back in the early 2000s. It proved extremely politically unpopular. No one was willing to make any sacrifices. Remember, it is human nature for people to refuse to make small sacrifices now, even if they are certain there will be dire consequences later. All of the solutions that were developed either involved somebody giving something up – or taking on more risk. Not much was resolved. The politicians decided to pick another issue to debate and life went on – but with no real solutions for the future of Social Security.

So, what does this mean for you? As you work, you will continue to pay into Social Security. The current retirees are dependent on you (remember – they are entitled). In fact, it wouldn't surprise me if Social Security taxes are raised, and you pay even more in as time goes on. However, I don't believe that you are going to get much back when you retire. Some estimates that I respect suggest that you might receive about one-third of what current retirees receive. You might think that at least that is "something", but an additional caveat is that you might not get these benefits until you are very old. The age at which retirees qualify for Social Security has been on the rise for younger people. It would not surprise me if you don't qualify for full Social Security benefits until you reach age 77 or older. To summarize – you will take care of others, but NO ONE IS GOING TO TAKE CARE OF YOU.

NOTE: *Impossible to see… the future is… I'm the first to admit that I could be wrong about these assumptions. But what if I'm not?*

It's time to go!

Let me be clear that I'm not trying to make you angry at

the baby boomers. Can you honestly tell me you wouldn't do the same thing in their position? They are simply benefiting from societal timing whereas you are not. Even with your future financial challenges, you may very likely have an easier time than your children. Do you think it is fair for them to be upset with you? What I am trying to do is stress to you the importance of acting now. It is terribly difficult to begin planning for something today that you won't use for forty years, but that is exactly what you need to do.

The good news

Remember Sue? She amassed an impressive amount of money with much less out-of-pocket savings than Bob. She was able to do this because her investment dollars were allowed to earn a "compounded" rate of return over a longer period of time. Einstein once playfully commented that *"compound interest was the greatest mathematical discovery of all time"*. Let's discuss briefly why Einstein was so impressed. Compound returns are simple yet powerful. When you invest, your account grows. Then, when it grows again, you get growth on your growth. The more growth you get on top of growth – the more powerful the result. I don't know if you will get my 1980s movie reference – but have you ever seen "Gremlins"? In the film, the way the gremlins increased their numbers so substantially was with the power of compounding. The gremlins just needed time. In fact, one of the keys to powerful compound returns is time. Fortunately (if you don't waste it by procrastinating) you've got time! When it comes to planning, time is a wonderful asset, but it is easily wasted. You must use the time you have wisely. So, let's get started!

♦ † ♦

♦ CHAPTER ONE ♦

STARTING YOUR CAREER

First things first… In order to be financially successful, you are going to need to earn an income. Unless you are planning a life of criminal activity (which I strongly advise against), the most popular way to earn consistent income is to simply get a job. For many, landing their first "real" job and beginning a career can be incredibly frustrating. I know it was for me. I had a very difficult time finding my first out-of-school job. Then, once I found one, it wasn't long before I despised it and found myself looking for a better opportunity. Hopefully, things will be different for you. In fact, some statistics suggest that they might.

While there are numerous articles about how often 20-somethings job hop, the truth of the matter is that today's 20-somethings change jobs less than 20-somethings in my day (the early 2000s). This may be due to several positive employment trends.

In order to attract the most qualified workers, many employers are attempting to provide enriching job designs and career opportunities that may better fit the needs of younger workers. In addition, arrangements like flex time (allowing you to choose your own hours) and telecommuting (working from home) are becoming much more popular and may lead to higher job satisfaction and a longer tenure at a specific employer. But how do you get an enriching job that meets your needs?

Education

You don't need much education to know that better jobs tend to go to those with higher educations. For the purposes of this chapter, I am assuming that you have recently completed the highest level of education you intend to obtain (at least for a while) and are ready to use the education you have completed to begin a career. If you are planning to go back to school one day, I'll have more advice for you in chapter nine.

However, "learning" doesn't have to start or stop with the pursuit of a degree. Successful people tend to adopt the mindset of becoming "lifelong learners". These self-motivated individuals make it a point to continue the pursuit of knowledge regardless of their formal levels of education. Depending on your career goals, there may be classes you can take, certifications you can earn, or books you can read, that increase your knowledge and help you advance your career. Even if you cannot find opportunities for learning in your respective field, engaging in any activity that expands your mind is a habit of a lifelong learner. You might attempt to learn the skills of a new sport, to play a musical instrument, or to speak a foreign language. Any attempt to engage in new activities could potentially aid you in not only your enjoyment of life, but in making you more marketable to a prospective employer. The benefits of this learning lifestyle may not be noticeable immediately, but they will definitely pay off over a career.

Experience

To many prospective employers, "experience" is as important (if not more important) than education. The prime example of an "experience" that often leads to a job in a desired career field is an "internship" – a position in a firm designed for a student or trainee for the simple purpose of gaining experience. While most organizations desire to obtain their interns from educational institutions, some businesses do not require it. If the firm in which you would most like to work will not hire you without more experience, it may be possible to contact the firm's human resources department to inquire about any internship opportunities. Even if the answer is "no", you have at least demonstrated to the firm a strong desire to learn their business – and that level of commitment cannot hurt.

If you are able to obtain an internship, most of them are for approximately 110 hours and they are typically spread out over several weeks or even months. If the internship is unpaid (which is likely) and you need income over this period, you may be forced to work another job while interning. This is likely to be a stressful period – but in the realm of it all – it is an extremely small price to pay for the dramatically increased chance of obtaining the job you want at the company you want.

NOTE: *I'll never forget the semester back in 2004 when I was taking four classes and teaching four classes for almost no pay. Every day I would gaze at the calendar and count the days before the end of the semester. However, this stressful season allowed me to obtain the job I wanted, teaching at the college I most desired.*

If you cannot obtain experience in your desired organization or even in your desired field, you may still be able to find opportunities to increase your experience in skillsets important to your career. If necessary, do some research to determine the important skills needed for the career path you desire. Then, get creative in thinking of the non-obvious ways you can develop those skills. For instance, if you need sales experience, consider helping out a non-profit with fundraising. If you need writing examples, create your own blog. If you need experience training others, consider becoming a Sunday School teacher or providing basic computer skills to the thousands of people who know a lot less than you about computers, perhaps at your local rescue mission. There are numerous opportunities to gain experience outside of "business" and most employers value these endeavors. I'm sure if you think about it, you have already developed other useful skills. You just need to find a way to express to your employer that you have the skills they are looking for – even without the professional experience. How do you do this? With a great resume and cover letter...

Your resume and cover letter

Before I settled into my current position, I used to do some of the hiring at my previous organization. I recall one instance when I received over 200 resumes for a single position. I was able to quickly rid myself of approximately one fourth of these resumes by simply going through them and looking for typos. If I found a typo, it did not matter to me the education and experience that the applicant possessed; I deleted it immediately.

I know this sounds laughably obvious – but you have to be sure your resume is free of typos and grammatical errors. When you apply for a job, expect that there are hundreds of other applicants out there who are after the same position and the person in charge of hiring is actively seeking reasons to toss out your resume that have nothing to do with your skills and qualifications (yet). A typo in your resume is an excellent way to be culled out immediately.

While a resume free from typos is a great start, it is also important to be sure that your resume is clean and professional-looking. Be sure to use a simple text style since many employers use software to initially scan your resume for typos and key words. In some cases, the software may not be able to read elaborate text styles (and your resume will be culled). However, after the initial screening, then you need some "guts" to your resume and cover letter that will impress a hiring manager, who is now paying attention to you. If you have recently graduated, you may find that your alma mater's career services department would be more than happy to help you develop a great resume full of "guts".

If obtaining assistance from your previous institution is not possible, there are many resources available to you on-line that can help you develop a professional-looking resume (perhaps even geared toward your desired industry). One of the best "free" resources available to you might be the "Career Services" page of your favorite local university. For instance, where I live, the University of Virginia is a popular and well-respected academic institution. Therefore, I just spent a few minutes searching their career services page and found a link to

"Resumes" that walks me through the following:

- How to start your resume
- Resume Builder
- Formatting your resume
- Resume examples

Each section is full of helpful information that is available to help anyone (not just students) develop a great looking resume. Further, I found resources on the same page that provide details on creating a professional cover letter. Your cover letter provides you with the means to draw attention to the items of your resume that you most wish to highlight. If you are serious about a position, be sure to write a cover letter that is carefully designed to highlight how your specific education and experience match the needs of the organization. You may need to do some research first, but a carefully-worded cover letter is much more liable to catch a hiring manager's attention over a "generic" cover letter that was obviously written in a manner that would allow it to quickly be sent to numerous employers.

I'm confident that if you check out a few university websites, and spend a few minutes perusing their career services pages, you will find information that will do an excellent job of helping you create a powerful resume and cover letter based on your education and experience. Even if you check the resources of two or three universities, it won't take you much time and best of all – it's free!

NOTE: *When I was trying to find my first real job, I felt that the resumes and cover letters I sent to prospective employers were flawless, but I heard back from laughably few. I couldn't understand why I was having such a difficult time! Now, many years later, if I could go back and give my younger self some advice in regard to my career, I'd strongly advise a more focused effort to build a network.*

Networking – the key to getting noticed

The easiest way to get your "foot in the door" at a prospective employer is to know someone who works there. If you are successfully "networked", then you have developed contacts with people at different organizations in which you can now exchange information. Much of the time, the exchange of information is in regard to careers and career development. Many jobs are simply not advertised. In order to apply for them, you HAVE to know someone at the organization. Further, you will be taken much more seriously as a candidate if someone in the hiring organization has "vouched" for you. According to the U.S. Bureau of Labor Statistics, approximately 70% of all jobs are found through networking. Other organizations estimate that the number may be closer to 85%. Regardless, it is important to constantly be building your network.

NOTE: *I've spoken to some young people who say they want to get hired "on their own merit". They want their education and experience to get them a job rather than the help of their family or friends. For the most part – this thinking is just dumb. Developing a network is a great skill! You should be proud that you have people willing to help you. Take advantage of it!*

It may be easiest for you to think of your network as both formal and informal. Formal networks are for the sole purpose of networking. Joining your local chamber of commerce is an example of an attempt to develop a formal network. Other examples may include professional organizations in your field or your school's alumni association. For the most part, the people you meet at these events are not your "friends" but are simply "friendly faces" who may be willing to exchange information with you. In some cases, formal networks may have fees or other dues and it is important to consider the cost/benefits of joining these networks. There is no doubt that a formal network is helpful, but in the long run, it may not be as useful as your informal network when it comes to finding a job.

You almost certainly have already developed a sizable informal network of friends and relatives. Informal networks can "just happen", but to effectively utilize your informal network takes work. Fortunately, social media has aided social networking immeasurably. Particularly, the social media site "LinkedIn" provides you with a wonderful way to grow and utilize your network. Many business professionals use LinkedIn to connect with others, build relationships, and maintain a network of vital business contacts. As such, it is highly recommended that you create a profile on LinkedIn that is meaningful and professional. Keep in mind that LinkedIn is for professionals only! Your efforts to find a job using LinkedIn can backfire if you treat it like many young people treat Facebook or Twitter.

If you are unfamiliar with LinkedIn, consider creating an account (www.linkedin.com) and spending a few moments acquainting yourself with its features. Once you begin to develop your profile, here are a few tips:

- Use a professional-looking photo – Professional dress, high resolution.
- Use the headline feature to inform your network that you are actively seeking employment.
- Think of the summary feature as a short cover letter. Draw attention to your qualifications and goals – but be brief.
- Recruiters actively seek candidates for open positions by searching for key words. Think about the key words that describe the position you want, and use them when describing your skills and experience.
- Search for friends and family whom you know well. Simply "invite" them to link in with you.
- Search for those acquaintances whom you may not know well, but may be good contacts for your job search. Rather than simply "inviting" them to link in with you, consider personalizing their invitation. Perhaps you will want to remind them of how you met, or inform them of your job search.
- Join groups of interest to you.
- Regularly update your status and share information and articles that relate to the career field that you would like to pursue.
- Consider asking for recommendations from those who have worked with you or who know you well. If someone grants your request, it is polite to ask them if you may write a recommendation for them as well.
- You may even consider posting your own original content. Write informative articles or create videos that relate to your chosen career field and post them on your profile page.

You should absolutely never post any questionable material on LinkedIn. Expressing your personality and sense of humor is great – but keep it professional! In fact, you should consider making this a rule for all of your social media (particularly Facebook). Potential employers will look for you on these sites and if you have posted material that makes them question your employability, they will quickly remove you from consideration! It would be a terrible shame if you had a contact at an organization who vouched for your character, and then that character is quickly refuted when a hiring manager simply checks your Facebook page and sees how proudly you display your middle finger.

In addition to keeping your social media accounts clean and professional, it is my strong advice to use any and all of your personal resources when job hunting. Your network wants to help you! Consider it this way – take a moment and think of someone you like and respect. If you could help them get a job in your organization, wouldn't you enjoy doing that? When it comes to networking, you will experience immense joy when your network helps you find a job and you will very likely also experience immeasurable joy when you later help someone in your network find a job. It's a win/win…

Don't give up hope

If you have been looking for work and have not yet met with success, you are not alone. Many recent graduates have suffered the same frustration. While easier said than done, it is terribly important to be patient and refuse to give up. Sometimes, graduates have no choice but to take jobs that are not in their chosen career field. If this is you, then know that it is only a rough season. A better season will come. It is important to do your best work - no matter what that work might be. Personally, I HATED my first job. To be completely honest, I didn't even really want to be a financial advisor, but it was the only job I could get! However, I look back on that experience and wouldn't change it for anything. I learned so much during that time, and now I am able to use that knowledge to do exactly what I enjoy. Don't lose hope, and with time, you may have a similar experience.

◆ † ◆

◆ CHAPTER TWO ◆

THE ENTREPRENEURIAL OPTION

In my classes, I talk a lot about Amazon. When teaching business and investing, there are very few companies that have better stories and provide better examples than Amazon.com. One of the great stories about Amazon (according to Business Insider) is the story of Jeff Bezos, its founder. Bezos, like many of us, worked in jobs he didn't like when he was young, but he ended up as a Senior Vice President of a successful hedge fund. This would have been the end goal for many of us – SUCCESS ACHIEVED! But Bezos had an overwhelming urge to leave the comfort of this high paying and relatively low stress job to start a risky Internet business (Amazon.com). In fact, shortly after the company went public in 1997, the firm was referred to by many investors as "Amazon.Bomb" because it, like numerous other Internet start-ups, was doomed for failure. But Bezos never gave up. He kept developing the company, and all the while, people kept buying from Amazon. Today, Bezos is one of the richest people in the world with a net worth over

$115 billion, and many people (myself included) admire the success of Amazon. Now… given this story, have you ever thought about starting your own business?

Many people your age have thought about entrepreneurship as a potential career option. However, very few recent graduates actually follow through with their entrepreneurial ideas. Typically, the logic is "I want to work for a company first. I need a steady paycheck. Let me make some money and get some work experience, and then I'll start my business."

I don't necessarily disagree with these thoughts, but let me give you another thought. If you wait… if you get a job and earn a steady paycheck… you will quickly get used to it. Before long, you won't be able to bear the thought of losing that paycheck. You (in essence) will become addicted to the paycheck. In addition, what else do you think is likely to happen over the next few years? Might you get married? Buy a house? Have a child or two??? Are you going to quit a steady paying job then? Probably not – and no one would blame you. It sounds a little irresponsible. So… given this logic… might now potentially be the best time in your life to start your own business?

Before you commit, know that it takes some special personal characteristics to be a successful entrepreneur. First, you need to have passion about a skill or product that you feel you can sell. Are you a good artist? Can you landscape or cut hair or crunch numbers with the best of them? Use your creativity. If you believe you have a product or skill that others would be willing to purchase from you, then the next step is to think through how you will get your product/service in front of them. How will they learn about your business and how can you convince them that they need it?

In addition to being passionate about your business idea, you need to be comfortable with risk. Being your own boss is pretty cool, but there is a lot of uncertainty. Before becoming successful, many entrepreneurs endure long periods of time without any certainty of a paycheck. This can be very stressful and the thought of simply working for someone else becomes very attractive.

Perhaps most importantly, you are going to need some "people skills". As a business owner, you will be dealing with other people. You will need to be persuasive and possess strong negotiation skills. You can't be overly aggressive with people, but at the same time, you can't be a pushover.

Do you think you have what it takes to be a successful entrepreneur?

If you value independence, flexibility, and taking on a challenge, but are still uncertain if entrepreneurship is for you then consider reading the following books:

- Think and Grow Rich by Napleon Hill,
- Rich Dad Poor Dad by Robert Kiyosaki,
- How to Win Friends & Influence People by Dale Carnegie, and
- Getting to Yes: Negotiating Agreement Without Giving In by Roger Fisher, William Ury, and Burce Patton

These books do a great job at helping the reader experience (albeit second-hand) what entrepreneurship feels like. Do you like these feelings? Or are you more interested in obtaining certainty and stability in your career? Perhaps you will find that you are attracted to the idea of starting your own business, but are reluctant to go "all in". If this is the case, it may still be possible to earn extra money by starting your own "side" business (a business you run in addition to holding a regular job). Regardless of the size and commitment, running your own business can be exciting and even quite fun. However, it will be challenging. Fortunately, there are lots of resources available to help you.

The Small Business Administration

The first stop for anyone interested in starting a business should be the Small Business Administration (SBA). You can check out their website at www.sba.gov. The mission of the SBA is to help Americans "start, build, and grow business". The SBA has page after page of information on how to start your business and they may even provide you with funds to help you get started. In addition to the website, you may find local offices called Small Business Development Centers (SBDCs) that provide hands-on assistance to current and prospective small business owners. There is an extensive list of all the local SBDCs available on the SBA website. Another free resource through the SBA is the Service Corps of Retired Executives (SCORE). This organization can provide you with counseling and advice from qualified (but frequently retired) volunteers.

Family and friends

You'd be surprised how many people have started a business. If you know anyone with their own business; talk to them. They may provide you with a wealth of practical knowledge about what worked. In addition, not to try to talk you out of your entrepreneurial dreams, but most start-up businesses fail. You may have a close family member who started a business 20 years ago and couldn't make it work. Talk to them too. You can learn a lot from talking to people about what didn't work. In fact, for those entrepreneurs who don't give up after their first business fails, the odds of a second business start-up succeeding are dramatically higher. While a failed first business is disappointing, you won't believe how much you learn from the experience.

These same family and friends may be excited about your new idea and want to help you. It doesn't sound very cool, but the most popular place to find investments or loans for your start-up business is from your own family and friends who are excited about your idea. Hopefully, you can obtain all the capital you need for your start-up from your own personal resources and those family/friends who believe in your business idea. However, if you still need more start-up capital to make your business a reality, the resources at the SBA may help you to find other potential investors including venture capitalists and angel investors.

Your local college or university

Entrepreneurship is currently one of the big important buzz words on many college and university campuses. There seems to be a push by the federal government to get more of you to start small businesses, which means schools can qualify for federal grants if they use the money for entrepreneurial programs. Many are growing and would like nothing better than to help you start your business. The potential options for help here are limitless. To find out what your school might do for you, look up the business department's homepage on your favorite college or university website. Look around and see if they have any programs that work with entrepreneurs from the community. If you don't see anything, contact the chairperson of the business department. It won't hurt to ask.

NOTE: *While the opportunities at every school will be different, at my college, we help many local entrepreneurs develop business plans for their start-up ideas. A business plan is a formal document that describes the concept of your business and outlines your business goals. It also provides details as to just how exactly you plan to achieve those goals – what it will cost and what you project to earn.*

Franchises

Franchises let you own and operate your own business, but don't make you start from scratch. You basically license with an already established (and hopefully successful) business model. There are likely hundreds of franchises that would be interested in opening up their business in your area, and typically, franchises have a much better chance of being successful than a business without a proven model. However, as always, there is a catch. First of all, the franchise is going to charge you a fee and require that you have a certain amount of cash before they will work with you. Some franchises are very expensive (with cash needs in the millions) while others do not have much initial cash need at all (perhaps as low as a few thousand dollars). It depends on the type of business. In addition, the franchise will want to be sure you are qualified to run their franchise before turning the keys over to you. This may involve an application process and sometimes a significant amount of training (at your expense). If you are interested in a franchise opportunity, check out www.franchise.com. This website provides you with some great insight into the franchises available to you and their costs to set up.

Once a small business is profitable…

Once your business is earning a profit, it's time to take advantage of some potential retirement savings opportunities. As a "small" business owner, you may not want to have the same types of retirement plans that larger organizations tend to prefer. The two most popular retirement benefit plans for small business owners are the SEP and the SIMPLE. Both these plans provide you with a way to save for retirement and provide some benefits to your employees that may increase their job satisfaction.

Simplified Employee Pension (SEP)

The SEP is for self-employed owners of small businesses and their qualified employees. To be qualified, the employees need to meet certain guidelines that the employer decides (but can only make so strict based on age, time of employment, and income earned).

The paperwork is incredibly simple, the employer just sets up an "IRA – an individual retirement account" for him/herself and all qualified employees. Contributions are then made by the employer and are income tax-deductible for the employer but are still subject to Social Security and Medicare taxes.

NOTE: Much more on setting up IRAs will come in chapter twelve.

The owner is allowed to contribute 25% of his/her compensation (up to a maximum dollar amount – but it is pretty high) to his/her SEP. But here is the catch… for whatever contribution the owner makes to his/her account; he/she must make the same percentage contribution to all eligible employees' SEP plans.

Example: Assume a small business with an owner and one employee. Owner's salary = $100,000 and the employee's salary = $30,000. The owner is allowed to save $25,000 into her SEP IRA (25% × $100,000) but then must also make a $7,500 contribution to the employee's SEP IRA (25% × $30,000).

Savings Incentive Match Plan for Employees (SIMPLE)

Another retirement plan option for small business owners (with 100 or fewer eligible employees) is the SIMPLE IRA. Just like the SEP, the SIMPLE has low administration responsibilities and is easy to set up. Once again, it's pretty much like setting up a traditional IRA, but with a higher allowed contribution ($12,500/year in 2018).

The catch for the SIMPLE is that the employer must match each eligible employee's contributions up to 3% or provide a flat 2% contribution regardless of employee participation. In this case, to be an eligible employee, one must only expect to earn at least $5,000 in compensation per year. The employee is vested in all contributions immediately – even if they quit or get fired. The employer's contributions are once again income tax-deductible.

Don't become a victim of success

These cool retirement plans are not generally the reason why young people become interested in entrepreneurship. Most recent graduates explore entrepreneurial endeavors because of their passion for the business and their desire for independence, flexibility and challenge. However, if you are one of the lucky few who enjoy success in your business start-up, please don't neglect planning for your future. Consider setting up one of these retirement plans and lower your current tax bill as well as increase your future financial security. Please see chapters eleven and twelve for more information on this topic.

Last word on start-ups

I'd wager that very few people who have started successful businesses really felt like they knew what they were doing when they took their first steps. Don't forego a lifelong dream because you are afraid you will fail. You very well may fail – and learn a lot from the failure. Then again, you could succeed… Just look at Jeff Bezos.

♦ † ♦

◆ CHAPTER THREE ◆

GET A HANDLE ON YOUR CURRENT SITUATION

Several years ago, I needed a place to keep my lawnmower, so I bought a garden shed from my local hardware store. It came in a kit that had all pre-cut wood, but putting it all together was going to be my job. I'd never done anything quite like this before, but I was fairly confident that I could put this thing together. Once the kit was delivered, I located a good spot for it in my yard, but the yard wasn't perfectly level. I figured I'd take an hour or so before getting started on the shed assembly to level out the yard a little bit. Four days of backbreaking work later, I had leveled out a space just big enough for my shed. Once the yard was level, the rest of the shed only took me about a day to complete.

My point in telling this story is that in order to build your successful financial future, you need to lay the foundation for it first. It would seem like building the shed would be the hard part – but it's really not. Getting yourself to a place where you can build is the hard part. My goal for writing the prologue of this book was to motivate you to act. Assuming you have found a way to earn consistent income, I hope you are motivated to save a whole bunch of money, invest it wisely and retire early. But we need to slow down and back it up a little here. Before we can do all that (we will get to it – I promise), we need to get a handle on your current situation.

To briefly revisit my story, I had difficulty leveling my yard for two primary reasons. The first reason was that I didn't really know what I was doing. The second reason was that I didn't have the right tools for the job. These two facts, taken together, made things very difficult for me. To prevent you from having the same analogous problems, in this chapter, we are going to learn how to get your financial foundation in place by using two great tools – a budget and a balance sheet. But before you get started, it is extremely helpful to do a little homework. Fortunately, it should be pretty easy. Just gather up all the documentation (either on-line or at home) of your financial life.

Here is a partial list of what I mean:

- Past bills (the more the better)
- Credit card statements (again, the more the better)
- Loan information (student loans, mortgages, auto loans, etc.)
- Income from your job (W2 statements)
- Any other income (interest/dividends you receive, regular gifts, capital gains, etc.)
- Bank statements (checking, savings, CD's)
- Any other assets you own (mutual funds, 401(k), IRA, stocks, bonds, real estate, etc.)

- List of insurance policies
- Benefit handbooks/statements from your employer

If you don't know what all of these items are – don't worry about it. Just get everything "financial" you can find. We will worry about what it is, and where it goes shortly…

Budget

Once you are armed with all of your financial information, the next step is to arrange it in an order that will be helpful to you for analysis. Let's start with the budget. A budget is simply an estimate of your inflows and outflows. We are going to use your information to determine the amount of money you have coming in and the amount you have going out. When it comes to creating a budget, you have several options. If you want to go completely old school, you could simply use a pencil and paper. However, given that your budget is a "living" document, it will continuously change. Therefore, it may be much simpler to use a spreadsheet like Microsoft Excel to maintain your budget. In addition, there are some free on-line budgeting tools that you may prefer. Personally, I really like Mint (www.mint.com). In addition, to budgeting tools Mint provides you with other helpful tools like bill tracking.

Income

Regardless of the budgeting tool you use, start with the money you have coming in. Take a quick peek at Exhibit 3-A for an idea of what a finished budget may look like. As far as income, you may have more (or less) sources of income than has been included in Exhibit 3-A, but it contains some fairly popular inflows (salary and gifts) as an example. Find all of your inflows and include them if you project to receive them over the next year. Notice that Exhibit 3-A lists both a "monthly" and an "annual" figure. This is recommended even if the particular item is on a different schedule. For instance, you may be paid every two weeks. If this is the case – you will need to do a little extra math.

Example: Let's assume you get paid every two weeks – and the amount is $923.08. Take this figure and multiply it by 26 (since you get paid 26 times per year). $923.08 × 26 = $24,000. Then divide the annual figure by 12 to get your "monthly" pay of $2,000.

NOTE: *Every two weeks is not the same as twice a month. If you get paid twice a month – your multiplier is 24 instead of 26. In the budgeting process, many people calculate this incorrectly – so be careful.*

Even if you only receive an inflow once a year, put this amount into both your annual and monthly budget columns. For all of your income and expenses that are not monthly – you will need to do the math to figure out what they are on a monthly and annual basis. This could take a little time, but it's worth it.

Savings

Next, we are going to look at any regular savings you have. If you don't regularly save anything (perhaps into a retirement plan or a savings account) then you can skip to the next section. Just to be clear, the term "savings" in this instance does not mean your savings account balance. If you have $1,000 in a savings account – that does not go here. What would go here is your regular savings into this account. In Exhibit 3-A, $10 per month is being saved into a piggy bank, but the amount that has already been saved into the piggy bank (the balance) is not listed here. We'll get to that later.

NOTE: *If you get your paycheck direct deposited into a checking account that you then use to fund your regular expenses, loans etc. – this doesn't count as savings. Don't put that here. Only put here regular savings that you don't regularly withdraw.*

Fixed expenses

Let's move on to your spending. We are first going to look at those expenses that you really don't have a lot of control over. They are outflows that are fixed and you can't easily modify them. Exhibit 3-A can get you started with some popular fixed expenses, but these are not all inclusive:

NOTE: *If you carry a balance on your credit card(s), then include credit card payments.*

If you pay off your credit card each month – then that makes me very happy! You would not need to list credit card payments as a fixed expense. Rather, list the separate items (groceries, gas, and the like) in which you use your credit card as a payment mechanism.

Variable expenses

The final category for your budget will be variable expenses. You will have at least some control over these expenses. You may not really feel like you do – but you do. You may have numerous other variable expenses based on your hobbies, interests, buying habits, etc. Be sure to catch them all. Looking over old credit/debit card statements may be a good way to find them.

> *NOTE:* *Many of these expenses may fluctuate substantially over the year. For instance, your utility bill may be $150 in February but only $50 in April. For these types of expenses, take the best "average" of them you can. For the utility bill example in Exhibit 3-A, $150 and $50 average out to $100. This is why it is good to have collected many of your old bills to help you estimate an accurate average number.*
>
> *Don't put too big of a number into the "Miscellaneous" category. Everybody has random things that occur (like an unplanned purchase of a personal finance book) that fit well into this category. But, if it is more than 10% of your income – you need to do some more digging and better understand the outflow.*

Putting it all together

Once you are satisfied that you have captured all of your income and expenses in your budget, now comes the moment of truth. Let's put it all together and calculate up the math to see what (if anything) you have left over. Subtract your savings and expenses from your income.

The goal of putting this budget together is to understand your inflows and outflows. Before you can save for the future, you need to know if you have anything that can be saved. If you have completed your budget and you have a positive number in the "Income – Savings/Expenses" calculation, then you have positive discretionary income (money left over that you can apply to your goals). It also means that you spend less than you make, which is a healthy financial habit.

However, notice in the case of Exhibit 3-A that the discretionary figure is negative. If you have negative discretionary income, then you are spending more than you make, and as of now, you do not have any additional savings capability. In fact, each month, you are digging yourself deeper into a financial hole. Do you remember the power of compounding that was discussed earlier? It works in reverse too! If you find that you have negative discretionary income, you are compounding yourself into financial ruin. You need to change this now! Older generations might be able to get away with some of this irresponsibility. They have you to help take care of them. No one is going to take care of you.

You may be wondering – "how is it even possible for me to spend more than I make". The answer is pretty simple – credit cards. You are charging more than you can afford to buy and (to be brutally blunt) you must stop. We are going to address the problem of credit cards more deeply in a later chapter. However, the basis of the problem is that you are spending too much. Either make more money or cut back on your spending.

EXHIBIT 3-A – Sample Budget

Item	Monthly	Annual
Salary	$2,000	$24,000
Support from grandma	$20	$240
TOTAL INCOME	**$2,020**	**$24,240**

Item	Monthly	Annual
401(k) savings	$100	$1,200
Savings into a piggy bank	$10	$120
TOTAL SAVINGS	**$110**	**$1,320**

Item	Monthly	Annual
Federal income tax	$200	$2,480
State income tax	$40	$480
FICA/FUTA	$30	$360
Mortgage (or rent)	$400	$4,800
Homeowners insurance	$20	$240
Property taxes	$20	$240
Student loan payments	$100	$1,200
Auto loan payments	$110	$1,320
Auto insurance premiums	$50	$600
Life insurance premiums	$5	$60
Health insurance premiums	$60	$720
Credit card payments	$50	$600
TOTAL FIXED	**$1,085**	**$13,020**

Item	Monthly	Annual
Groceries	$250	$3,000
Gifts to others	$20	$240
Utilities (Gas, Water, Elect)	$100	$1,200
Phone	$80	$960
Cable/Internet	$120	$1,440
Eating out	$200	$2,400
Transportation	$50	$600
Misc.	$100	$1,200
TOTAL VARIABLE	**$920**	**$11,040**

INCOME – SAVINGS/EXPENSES	- $95	- $1,140

Even if you have positive discretionary income – it is better to have more! Everyone can benefit from earning extra income or cutting back on their expenses. There are numerous books on the topic. One of my favorite authors on this topic is Clark Howard. You can also get tips from his regular radio show. However, here is a brief overview of some expense cutting possibilities:

- Get rid of cable/satellite and even streaming services until you can better afford them.
- Eat at home instead of a restaurant and brew your own coffee.
- Pack your lunch (from experience I can state this has a huge positive impact on your finances).
- Shop around for better insurance rates (car, homeowners, etc.). Try bundling discounts when possible.
- Turn up/down the thermostat and either get a blanket or a fan.

- Walk places when you can (instead of driving) and consider using public transportation instead of owning a car.
- Don't get a new pet until you know you can afford it.
- If possible – do it yourself (home/car maintenance, grooming, food preparation, etc.)
- With the possible exception of some on-line purchases - if something you are buying is convenient – then there is probably a less expensive alternative that is not as convenient.
- You probably have enough electronics, shoes, and clothes for a while. You don't have to have the latest and greatest "everything".
- Find and use coupons.

  Consider using phone apps that can help you save money on purchases you are already making. Take a look at "Ibotta" (www.ibotta.com) for some potentially awesome rebates, and also check out "RetailMeNot" (www.retailmenot.com) for some great coupons and promo codes. Do some investigating, there may be more apps out there that can better help you save based on your buying habits.

  BUT BE CAREFUL! You are not saving money buying something "on sale" or with a coupon that you wouldn't have purchased otherwise. That's an excuse!

- Use common sense and be creative. I'm sure if you really thought about it, you could think of ten ways right now that you could reduce your expenses that have not been mentioned.

Cutting back on expenses is both an action and a process. It is difficult to do it all in one day. Do what you can today, and continue to work on it over time. The higher you are able to make your discretionary income (money left over), the more you are going to be able to save. The more you can save, the better your chances of financial success.

Once you begin to feel pretty good about your budget; it is completely okay to treat yourself every once in a while. You don't want to go through life never enjoying anything. It is important to "occasionally" do something unplanned and frivolous that you enjoy – but use discretion (and the common sense mentioned earlier).

Balance sheet

With the budget, we created an estimate of your household inflows and outflows for the upcoming month and year. Now, with the balance sheet, we are going to take a snapshot of your current financial position. Your balance sheet will list your assets and liabilities (debts). When you subtract what you owe from what you own, you get your net worth. Let's start with your assets. Assets can be classified into three categories: liquid, investment, and personal.

Liquid assets

Liquid assets are assets that can quickly be converted into cash (cash is arguably the most liquid asset). Most (but not all) liquid assets are held at a bank like your checking and/or savings account balances. Other liquid assets might be certificates of deposit and money market accounts. Note that on the balance sheet, we are not looking for the "savings" number that you entered into the budget – but the current balance of the account.

Investment assets

Investment assets are typically considered to be assets that are for some future goal (over 5 years). You can convert them into cash fairly easily, but you may not want to... Consider being forced to sell a stock on a day when the market has been hit hard – and your stock is substantially lower than the day before. You could do it, but you would probably rather wait. An additional characteristic of investment assets is that they generally have the potential for higher returns than do liquid assets. This will be discussed in much greater detail in chapter eleven.

Investment assets can further be broken down into retirement and non-retirement assets. Popular retirement assets include: Traditional and Roth individual retirement account (IRA), 401(k), 403(b), 457 plans and Simplified Employee Pensions (SEP). Other popular non-retirement investment assets are stocks, bonds, mutual funds, real estate, and rental property.

NOTE: *If you have retirement assets, they will likely be invested in stocks, bonds, mutual funds, etc. They may even be invested in "liquid" assets. The fact that they are held in a "retirement plan" simply means that you have a metaphorical umbrella over the asset that protects it from being taxed. There will be more on this topic in chapter twelve. For now, be sure you do not double count these assets. List them under retirement investment assets only.*

Personal assets

Personal assets are assets that you may use in your daily life. They could be things like: collections, cars, clothing, your home, household furnishings, etc. You will need to develop your own dollar value for many of these assets.

NOTE: *Many people place way too high a value on their personal items. Remember, it's only worth what someone will pay you for it – not what you paid for it. As soon as you wear that $200 jacket for the first time, it drops in value. If you are honest with yourself, you might get $20 for it in a yard sale (or maybe less). Be fair and truthful with your valuations.*

Liabilities

After listing your assets (what you own), you are going to switch to what you owe. It's easier if you list your debts as short-term and long-term. The idea behind short-term debt is that you are going to pay it off soon (within one year). These debts may include your credit card balance. If student loans are due within a year, you would put the balance of these loans here too. Long-term debts will take you a year or longer to pay off (mortgages, auto loans, some student debts, etc.). Balances for all these items can usually be found on your bill or invoice.

Net worth

Once you have found the values of all your assets and listed the balances of all your debts, you are ready to build your balance sheet and discover your net worth. An example of a completed balance sheet might look like Exhibit 3-B:

EXHIBIT 3-B – Sample Balance Sheet

Liquid Assets	
Checking	$2,500
Savings	$4,000

Investment Assets	
Stock mutual fund	$3,000
401(k)	$10,000

Personal Assets	
Residence (home's current value)	$200,000
Automobile	$12,000
Coin collection	$500
Household items	$1,000

TOTAL ASSETS	$233,000

Current Liabilities	
Credit card balance	$5,000

Long-term Liabilities	
Mortgage (principal remaining)	$180,000
Auto loan (principal remaining)	$5,000
Student loan (principal remaining)	$10,000

TOTAL LIABILITIES	$200,000

NET WORTH	$33,000

In this example, the net worth of this individual is a positive $33,000. If this person is 20 years old – then it is awesome! However, if this person is 40 years old, then this is quite sad. However, it could be worse. Some people have a negative net worth. In fact, as a recent graduate, your net worth is liable to be negative if you have student loans. These loans have no offsetting asset (except hopefully for your increased potential to earn money). If you are recently graduated with student loans, and your net worth is negative – this is not that big of a deal (yet). If you still have a negative net worth five to ten years after graduation, then you may want to worry.

Regardless of the size of your net worth, the goal is to grow it. This first net worth calculation is your starting point. In fact, this is your main measure for financial success. It is recommended that you calculate your net worth at least once a year to see if you are growing financially. If you are stalled out – then that is a red flag and you need to make some changes. Re-read this book and follow the recommendations. If you are responsible and make smart financial choices, you can't help but to grow your net worth over time and significantly increase your chances of financial success.

♦ † ♦

♦ CHAPTER FOUR ♦

BANKING & SAVING

Dealing with a bank (like your budget) is an on-going process. If you do not already have a bank account, you need one. Unfortunately, it is likely that as a recent graduate, the bank is going to have much more negotiating power than you. So, shop around for the best deal today, but keep in mind that today's "best" deal may not remain the best deal once you earn a reputation for being financially responsible and build the size of your account. As you become more successful, you will likely want to continue to shop around and renegotiate with your bank to obtain and keep the absolute best deal. With your financial success over time, the tables can turn. Banks will want your business, and you will have more power in the negotiation. Keep this in mind as you read this chapter. As a brand new account holder, you may feel like the bank is taking advantage of you. You may have to take it, but just for a while… Continue to do the right things by keeping to your budget and making responsible financial decisions. Then, later, you may find the banks to be more cooperative, and even competing for your banking business.

When shopping around for a bank, you need to think about what banking features are most important to you, and do your research. There will likely be some tradeoffs and while I'll hit the high points with you, the bulk of the legwork must be done on your part. I'm also only going to discuss with you two of the most well-known establishments for banking services (commercial banks and credit unions). There are other types of financial institutions that perform similar services, but banks and credit unions are very popular, and I'm sure you will have many options between the two in your area. However, before we get into some specifics, let's first discuss why you must have a bank or credit union account. First off, aside from a company sponsored retirement plan, if you want to do anything cool like invest in the stock market, then you will need to contact an investment company to open up your own brokerage account. You can't really do this without a bank account first. Depending on the broker, it may be possible, but in my experience, brokerages are going to insist you fund your brokerage account from a pre-existing bank account. Brokerage houses are scrutinized heavily by regulatory agencies to ensure they don't help you engage in an activity known as "money laundering". If you already have a bank account, the brokerage is much less likely to be helping you launder terrorist or drug money and will be much more willing to work with you. But perhaps more important is the fact that if you are paid by check (and most of us are) then you need to convert that check into something useful, like cash. How might you do that if you don't have a bank account?

Check cashing services

If you are using a check cashing service, you are getting ripped off. I've seen some check cashing services that cost $15 to cash a $1,000 check. This is ridiculous. Banks are heavily scrutinized for their fees, but check cashing service fees are almost always significantly higher. If (for whatever reason) you cannot open a bank account, then the check cashing services at 7-11 or Wal-Mart may be your best bet. However, you may have additional options in your area that better meet your needs. It is important to shop around and get the best deal you can find. But as long as you are shopping around, why not check out some banks and credit unions? A much better deal is likely available. Let's get you started with some background on these establishments.

Banks

The technical term in the financial community for a bank is a "commercial bank". The names of these banks seem to change often with mergers and takeovers, but some of the popular names today are: Bank of America, SunTrust, Wells Fargo, JP Morgan Chase, Citi Group, and BB&T to name a few. You will also have much smaller, less popular local community banks that are specific to your area. For instance, where I live, a community bank is the Bank of Botetourt. Some people find that community banks have lower fees and are just plain friendlier than the larger banks. Obviously, your personal experiences may differ, but this is the general reputation. The biggest downside to a local bank is the lack of convenience. If I'm vacationing in Florida, where am I going to find a Bank of Botetourt ATM? The most convenient one is 700 miles from me. Compare that to the closest SunTrust ATM... That one is likely only a few blocks away.

Regardless of the size, these commercial banks all provide a full range of services including checking, savings, and lending. These banks also typically have their own financial advisory units (more on this in chapter thirteen).

Credit unions

To try to list the popular credit unions would be a difficult task. They are numerous, and many are specific to areas and/or professions. However, credit unions provide many of the same services as commercial banks, oftentimes at a lower cost. You can recognize them easily, because most have "credit union" in their name. Credit Unions arguably have less regulatory red tape than commercial banks, and thus can service clients and still earn a profit with lower fees. Anecdotally, I personally get a different "feel" from my credit union than I do from my commercial bank. The credit union really does seem to be more community-oriented rather than profit-oriented, which I believe is one of their goals. This may be because credit unions are also user-owned. This means that if you have an account at a credit union, you are part owner of that credit union. In the realm of it all, this is not that big of a deal, but it's kind of cool, I guess. One thing that is a little "off" about credit unions is that they call accounts by different names. I don't know why – I guess just to be different. For example:

- A checking account is called a "draft account" at a credit union.
- A savings account is called a "share account" at a credit union.

Both commercial banks and credit unions are viable options to use for your banking and savings needs. However, your personal preference for one or the other may be based on many factors. Therefore, let's discuss the types of accounts you might need and the factors involved. Once you are able to identify what is important to you, your preference for one bank versus another bank versus a credit union may become clear.

NOTE: *Going forward in this chapter, I'm only going to use the word "bank" when discussing the factors; however, please know that "bank" really means all types of banks and credit unions.*

Checking accounts

Checking accounts are very liquid (easily convertible to cash). When you open up a checking account, you typically have to buy "checks" (though sometimes they may be free – it depends). You can then write checks from your very own checkbook as payment at most establishments and use them similarly to cash. When the business you write the check to "cashes" your check, the money is removed from your account and put in the business' account. You can also link your debit or credit card to your checking account and pay in a similar fashion with the card (for more information on debit and credit cards, see chapter eight). Also, as I stated earlier, if you want to invest, your investment company will likely insist on a check (or a wire from your checking account).

When you get paid, you may have the option of having your employer directly deposit your paycheck into your checking account (or savings account for that matter). Banks generally like this, and may give you a better deal if you agree to direct deposit. However, if you are old fashioned, you can still fill out a deposit slip and walk it in to give to a bank teller to be deposited. If you are on the cutting edge, some of the larger banks even have "mobile deposits" that you can use on your smart phone. You just snap a couple of pictures of your check, fill in a few blanks on the phone app, and your check is deposited. In fact, one of the more convenient features of larger banks is their on-line deposit and bill pay services that link directly to your checking account. Once you get the on-line bill pay set up, you can generally pay all your bills every month quite effortlessly. Smaller banks may provide these options as well. If you like the mobile/on-line features, and also like a local community bank – ask them about their on-line and mobile capabilities. They may have what you need.

If personal service is not what you are after, and all you care about is working with a bank via your smart phone and/or computer – there are completely on-line banks that tend to offer good terms and special deals. This may be a desirable option if you prefer working entirely on-line, thus minimizing your contact with other humans. On-line accounts could arguably be difficult to obtain as your first bank account. The ones I've seen appear to insist on a check to fund your initial deposit. However, most have toll free numbers on their websites, so if you desire an on-line account, call them and see what options you have.

Once you have your checking account, you must be responsible! You cannot write checks that your account can't cash. Never let yourself get in a position where you are worried that a check might "bounce". Your bank will not be happy, and when banks get unhappy, they charge you fees. Most banks offer a feature known as overdraft protection. The way overdraft protection actually works may not be the way that it sounds like it works. If you feel you are at risk of bouncing a check and are tempted by the overdraft protection offered by your bank – be sure you understand what you are getting. It's not free. It's better to be so fiscally responsible that overdraft protection isn't an issue for you. I know this is easier said than done for some, but if this is a problem, you really need to re-read the section from chapter three on budgeting, and change your habits.

Savings accounts

Some banks call their savings accounts "passbook" accounts. Typically, savings accounts are a little less liquid than checking accounts, but pay slightly higher interest. Some "regular" savings accounts will link to your checking account (and is one of the ways overdraft protection may work) and may even come with their own ATM card, making them almost as liquid as checking accounts. "High interest" savings accounts usually have high minimum balances but pay higher interest than other types of savings accounts. When assessing a savings account, look for higher interest, lower fees (preferably none) and the ability to link your savings to your checking account. Savings accounts are designed to help you do just that – save. The thinking is that you would only put money into a savings account that you didn't plan to spend anytime soon (i.e. save it).

I've actually never had a savings account. I use a different vehicle (known as a money market fund) at my brokerage to meet my needs for a savings account, though I'm not necessarily suggesting you do the same. I'll discuss this option in greater detail in the next chapter; however, it is worth noting that my money market mutual fund is not "insured" like most savings accounts. Most bank accounts are insured by the Federal Deposit Insurance Corporation (FDIC) for up to $250,000. This means that if the bank fails, the federal government promises to step in and give you back any money you may have lost up to $250,000. I doubt you will be bumping up against this limit anytime soon, but if you have more than $250,000 and want FDIC insurance on all of it, the limit is per bank. The insurance that credit unions carry is the National Credit Union Share Insurance Fund (NCUSIF) and works very similarly to FDIC. Most banks and credit unions have the fact that they have this insurance prominently displayed somewhere in the bank and on the description of your account.

Other factors to consider

The first thing you will need to open a bank checking or savings account is money. Most banks have a minimum balance requirement. These minimum balances can vary significantly from bank to bank. There is generally a tradeoff here. The larger the minimum balance, typically the better the interest rate or the lower the fees associated with the account. Let's define these terms:

Minimum balance

A minimum balance is a dollar amount that you have to maintain in the account. Some of the cooler banking features like on-line bill pay may be free if you maintain a high enough balance. If this is important to you, be sure to ask. Of note, checking accounts typically have a minimum balance while many savings accounts do not (or have a minimum balance that is very low).

Example: Your bank's checking account might have a $500 minimum balance. As long as you have $500 or more in the account, the bank is happy. However, if you write too many checks and the account balance drops below $500, the bank is not happy. Remember what happens when banks get unhappy? They charge you a fee. My take on this particular banking practice is that it is a necessary evil. It is up to you to be responsible and not let your account dip below the minimum level.

Service fees

Service fees (or charges) at banks vary substantially. Some accounts might have a service charge every month, regardless of how much money you maintain in the account. I'm not a fan of these – even if they are very low. My personal rule of thumb here is that I dislike it when banks take my money way more than I like it when they pay me money. If I had any negotiating power at all, I would make every effort to find an account that had no regular service fees irrespective of my minimum balance. My strong advice is that you should do the same. If a bank is going to charge you a service fee because of some other feature you enjoy (like on-line access or ATM use) then that is a slightly different story – but once you have some reputation and funds, you should be able to have these fees waived as well. In addition to regular service fees, banks may have fees for all types of other services. If you think you are going to use a particular service often, try to find a bank that has a low (or no) fee for it. If you are not going to use it often (or ever) then who cares if they have a high fee?

Let me tell you a quick story to exemplify my point. Several years ago, my wife and I were buying a new house, and I needed a cashier's check from both my commercial bank and my credit union. A cashier's check is a special type of check that has been guaranteed by a financial institution and is typically needed for very large purchases. Anyway, at the credit union – they gave me one for free. I was pretty happy about that as normally cashier's checks have a fee associated with them; but they waived it. Then with a big smile on my face, I drove to my commercial bank. They told me there would be a $10 fee for a cashier's check. This is about what I expected so I got out $10 to pay the fee. "BUT WAIT!!!" said the teller. "If you change your account to our new and improved super deluxe account, we can waive that fee for you! Would you like to switch?" I thanked her for the offer, but respectfully declined. I've gotten maybe three cashier's checks over the course of my whole life. Who knows what other fees I would have been signing up for just to get free cashier's checks (that I almost never use)... And unlike you, I was unwilling to do my due diligence that day and really make an effort to understand all of the features and fees associated with the account that they wanted me to switch into... However, my experience with banking suggested to me that this wasn't going to be a good deal for me.

Interest bearing accounts

Some accounts (especially savings accounts) have interest rates. An interest rate is a good thing for "savers". This is the way the bank pays you for allowing them to use your money. In today's interest rate environment however, the interest rates that banks pay is so low, that they are almost non-existent (I think mine is currently .001% per month). Regardless of the amount, I generally like earning interest, but not as much as I dislike paying fees. If I had the option to earn interest and there were no fees – I'd take it. I'd even be willing to perhaps make a larger deposit for a higher interest rate. But in my experience with banking, it is almost always better to focus on minimizing fees over earning higher interest.

Seriously, interest rates are so low right now – why bother? Invest your money elsewhere where you have the opportunity to earn something more than pennies. (Much more to come on this topic in chapters eleven and twelve)

Be sure you get answers

Before pulling the trigger and deciding on your bank and account, be sure you have found sufficient answers to the following questions:

- Does this account have a regular service fee? If so, how much is it? Is there any way to have this fee waived?
- What is the minimum balance?
- What is the fee if I drop below the minimum balance?
- Is there overdraft protection? If so, how does it work? What does it cost?
- What other fees does this account have?
- How much is the fee for checks (if a checking account)?
- Is there another account that I may qualify for that has lower fees?
- Does this account pay interest? If so, how much?
- Is this account FDIC insured (if a bank) or insured by the NCUSIF (if a credit union)?
- What features does this account provide?
  - ATM access?
  - Debit card?
  - On-line bill pay?
  - Mobile deposits?
- Is there a fee for any of these features? If so, how much?
- Are there any limits to these features? (perhaps a limit to the number of accesses of the ATM per month)
- What is the fee if I go over the limit for the feature?

If you aren't really a people person, you may be able to find the answers to many (if not all) of these and other questions by doing your research on-line. However, if you need any clarification, I strongly suggest you ask an actual banking representative. It's their job to help you! If in asking your questions, there is anything you don't understand, make sure to get the banking representative to clarify it until you are sure you understand it. Most of all - don't be afraid to look stupid. The banker doesn't care if you are smart. I have personally asked a teller to explain something to me "as if I was 5 years old". There is no need to try to impress the banker with how quickly you grasp concepts and banking jargon. Ask and ask and ask again until you understand – and get it in writing!

Opening an account

When you decide on your bank and the type of account, opening it is fairly easy. If you have saved enough cash to make the minimum deposit, take it to your bank and ask a teller if you can talk to someone about opening an account. The teller may be able to help you, or they may find you another bank representative with whom you can sit and talk. Ask your questions and get sufficient answers from them. The people you talk to should be extremely friendly. If they act like you are a nuisance – then that is a red flag!

The account representative will likely do some quick tests on your cash to be sure that it isn't counterfeit, and the rest of the paperwork is fairly simple as long as you can prove you are who you say you are. The best way to prove this is with a driver's license. If your driver's license has your address on it, then that is likely going to be enough; however, to be on the safe side, you may want to bring a bill or some other documentation that has both your name and address on it.

If you want to open up your account with a check, the bank will be happy to work with you here too. Unless the check is a paycheck or a government issued check, the bank may want to place a temporary "hold" on it, restricting you from accessing it for a short while. This is normal so don't get worried. The bank just wants to be sure that your check is good before they allow you to withdraw it. If you are opening your account with a check, it may be possible to do it entirely on-line, but I highly suggest you visit the bank in person, regardless.

Of special note: If you are opening up an account with cash and/or your regular paycheck, you may have an additional option to meet the minimum deposit. Some banks will allow you to have your minimum deposit requirement met, even if you do not have enough initially, if you sign up for direct deposit. If this might be an option that could benefit you, be sure to discuss it with your banking representative.

♦ † ♦

♦ CHAPTER FIVE ♦

MAINTAINING A RAINY-DAY FUND

A lot of people (young and old) just can't seem to get ahead financially. Financial advisors hear the same story from many of their *less financially successful* clients – "Every time I manage to save up a little bit, something comes along to take it!"

No one can completely escape from bad luck – and neither will you. You may experience any or all of these examples:

- Your water heater will die.
- Your rent will increase.
- You will need to replace your home's roof.
- Your car will need work.
- You will lose your job.

I could list a thousand more examples of how something unexpected and unwelcome will come along to deprive you of your money. It is just a fact of life. Therefore, given that these things WILL happen, isn't it really kind of dumb to be surprised by them? The fact is that while it sounds like a good excuse, people who have this problem are simply spending too much. Please don't let this be you! Consider the advice and guidance provided in chapter three on spending and budgeting. Make sure you have discretionary income so that you can plan for these unexpected, but certain, expenses.

In fact, planning for life's rainy days is so important that it should actually be your first "investment" priority. If you have no savings to meet these unfortunate and unexpected occurrences, then your first financial goal should be to create a rainy-day or "emergency" fund. Consider dedicating almost all of your monthly discretionary income to just this one goal until it is met. After you have a sufficient emergency fund, then it will make sense to begin addressing your longer-term goals.

How much money should I keep in an emergency fund?

Because of the nature of emergencies, you want your emergency fund to be extremely liquid (easily convertible into cash). Unfortunately, by their nature, liquid assets typically do not earn much interest (or provide you with much return on your investment). Therefore, while you need an emergency fund, it doesn't make sense for it to be egregiously large. You have other longer-term financial goals that require funds as well, and you will likely want higher growth opportunities for these dollars (see chapters eleven and twelve for more information).

The typical advisor-recommended size of an emergency fund is three to six months' worth of your budgeted expenses. To understand your monthly expenses, simply re-visit the budget you created (based on the recommendations of chapter three). If you have a more "aggressive" mindset, you may only want to keep three months' worth of expenses in your emergency fund. If you are more "conservative" then you may be more comfortable keeping six months' worth of expenses in these liquid dollars. For a numerical example, if you spend roughly $2,000 per month on your regular expenses, then a three-month emergency fund would be $6,000 while a six-month emergency fund would be $12,000.

NOTE: *When determining the size of your emergency fund, consider the financial impact of losing your job. How long might it take you to find other work? In addition, consider the size of your emergencies. For example, the replacement parts of a Toyota are a lot less expensive than the equivalent parts on a Lexus. Use your judgement and maintain an emergency fund sizable enough to meet your needs. Six months' expenses may not be enough!*

      As you attempt to build an emergency fund, you may have emergencies that come along and deplete your hard-earned savings. If this is the case, do your best to pay for what you need, and then continue your effort to build an adequate emergency fund. I hate to keep harping on the need to cut expenses while attempting this endeavor, but it is really the most logical way to help most people meet their goal and move toward financial success.

Options for your emergency fund dollars

If your emergency fund goal is relatively small (say $5,000 or less) then you will probably just want to keep your funds easily accessible in a bank checking/savings account. However, if you need to maintain a larger fund, then you may want to consider other options. While the liquid assets typically used for an emergency fund suffer from extremely low rates of return, some of these assets do pay higher rates of interest than others. For instance, money market accounts are interest-bearing accounts you can purchase at your bank that generally pay higher interest than a bank savings account. The bank will lend out the money you save into these accounts as short-term loans to other borrowers (usually the government or large corporations). The tradeoff is that most money market accounts require you to maintain a higher minimum balance than a typical checking or savings account. For instance, many money market accounts may require you to maintain a minimum balance of $2,500, though some may be much higher (you will need to check with your bank).

NOTE: *Your bank may provide you the option of saving into a "money market account" or a "money market mutual fund". They are basically the same thing, but if you do some investigating, you may find that the money market mutual fund has historically paid a slightly higher rate of interest than the money market account. This is due to the fact that money market accounts are typically FDIC insured and money market mutual funds are not.*

Another popular emergency fund savings option is the certificate of deposit (or CD for short). This is a special note from a bank in which they will promise to pay you a stated level of interest on your money after a specified time period. Generally, a CD will pay a higher rate of interest than bank checking/savings and even money market accounts. However, CDs are somewhat less liquid in that you are restricted from taking any money out of your CD until the end of the stated time period. Early withdrawals will most likely incur a hefty fee.

NOTE: *If the bank is FDIC insured, any money you put into a CD (up to $250,000) will be FDIC insured as well.*

You are generally able to purchase CDs for almost any amount ($100 to $1,000,000). In addition, the maturity dates of CDs vary widely, but most often range between one month and five years. Longer-term CDs will invariably pay a higher rate of interest than shorter-term CDs. As an example, assume you are thinking of investing $1,000 into a CD. A six-month CD might pay you $100 at the end of six months whereas a one-year CD might pay you $235 at the end of a year. The tradeoff is relatively obvious. If you want to earn a higher return, you need to be willing to part with your money for a longer period of time.

Laddering CDs

One trick to increasing the liquidity of CDs is to "ladder" them rather than invest a lump sum into a single CD. For instance, assume that it is January, and you desire to invest $12,000 into a CD. You might struggle with the choice between a six-month and a one-year CD. The one-year CD pays higher interest, but it is less liquid. You could potentially have to wait an entire year to get your money back (without incurring a penalty). The six-month

CD, on the other hand, is twice as liquid, but the interest rate is substantially lower.

To adopt a laddering strategy with your CD investing, simply invest a portion of your money on a regular basis over a period of time. For instance, in the above example, you might choose to invest only $1,000 into a one-year CD in January. Then, in February, you invest an additional $1,000 into a one-year CD. Invest another $1,000 in March and so on. By the end of the year, you have invested the entire $12,000 and you will have $1,000 (plus interest) coming due each month. If you need the cash, you can take it, but if you don't need the cash, simply inform the bank to reinvest the money into another one-year CD.

A laddering strategy helps you to earn a higher rate of return by investing in longer-term CDs while increasing your liquidity in that you will always have a CD maturing each month.

Making the most of your emergency fund - the three-tiered strategy

Given that money markets and CDs are less liquid, but earn a higher rate of return than most checking and savings accounts, some investors tier their emergency funds to provide them with the best of both worlds.

There is no rule that says your emergency fund needs to be in the same account. Therefore, why not put some of your emergency fund dollars into highly-liquid (but low-interest) accounts and other dollars into higher-interest (but less liquid) accounts? Consider the benefits of a three-tiered emergency fund strategy with dollars in checking, a savings/money market account, and CDs.

As an example, assume that Alex has recently started a career in Washington D.C. With his relatively high rent, his living expenses average approximately $3,000 per month, and he desires to maintain an emergency fund equal to six months of his regular expenses. Alex may choose to only maintain $6,000 (two months' expenses) in his checking account. This is his most liquid account and the one he will utilize first in the event of an emergency. It is his hope that this account will cover the majority of his "emergency" needs. However, he also keeps another $3,000 (one month of expenses) in a money market account. This account has an investment minimum of $3,000 but pays higher interest than his checking account. He can liquidate it (convert it into cash) anytime, but it would require either a trip to the bank or a few taps on his bank's phone app. Lastly, Alex maintains $9,000 (three months' expenses) in "laddered" CDs. He invests $750 into a one-year CD every month. He hopes he never has to use this money and can simply reinvest each CD as it comes due. However, if he does need additional liquidity, he knows he has a CD coming due every month.

The first step to financial success

Just like any journey, the road to financial success begins with a single step. Some recent graduates may not be ready to take a step yet. If you have an overabundance of expensive debt, then you may find yourself in a financial hole. You need to climb out of the hole before you take any steps (more on this topic later). However, if you don't find yourself in a hole and simply want to begin making some sound financial moves that can lead to your eventual financial success, then building an adequate emergency fund is the first step in the right direction.

EXHIBIT 5-A – Sample Three-tiered Emergency Fund

Tier One Checking Account	Tier Two Money Market Account	Tier Three Laddered CDs
$6,000 Two months' expenses	$3,000 One month of expenses	$9,000 Three months' expenses
Lower Return/Higher Liquidity	Moderate Return/Moderate Liquidity	Higher Return/Lower Liquidity

At this point in your financial life, simply building an adequate emergency fund may feel impossible. It's not. If you prioritize the effort to save for this goal, you can make it happen. Perhaps you can only save $10 per month... That's awesome! Do it! If you can save $10 per month for a year – then you will have $120 that you wouldn't have had if you hadn't prioritized that savings. Please don't become overwhelmed with how big the goal is – and how little you seem to be contributing to it. Just save! If it bothers you that you are not making sufficient progress, don't give up! Cut your expenses and save more! Your accounts will grow and you will be moving toward your eventual financial success. This is a financial marathon – not a sprint!

♦ † ♦

◆ CHAPTER SIX ◆

AN OVERVIEW OF TAXES

I bet some of you are wondering if you should maybe skip this chapter… Just give me these two paragraphs to try to convince you why you shouldn't. First off – it's not that long! In this chapter, I only want to be sure that you understand enough about taxes so that you can try to take steps to minimize them. I'm not trying to make you a tax expert. I'm not one myself. I would; however, like to help you know what you are talking about as you meet with your tax accountant or income tax preparer.

Perhaps more important is the fact that smart financial planning will consider the implications of taxes. Proper tax planning in your investment strategy could make a difference of thousands of dollars of growth over your lifetime. I just want to be sure you don't miss out on that! However, in order to accomplish this, you really need an overview of some taxes. Fair enough?

Why do we pay taxes?

As a society, many of us use goods and services that need funding, maintenance, etc. Given the type of good or service, it just makes sense that a consolidated governing body does the upkeep (an example might be roads). The governing body will thus need to collect from us the money to do what they need to do. These are taxes.

The two primary political parties, Democrats and Republicans, are constantly negotiating the "right" amount of taxes to be collected. While this is hugely oversimplified, the Democratic Party is represented by people who would like to see greater tax revenues (to pay for more government services) while the Republican Party is represented by people who would like to see less tax collected (paying for less government services). Depending on what party has greater power in Washington will sometimes largely influence the level of taxes imposed on the American public. Regardless, the method for "who pays what and how much" is very complicated. To get us started, let's define two broad types of taxes.

Flat tax

A flat tax is fairly simple. Everybody pays the same rate or percentage. An example of a flat tax might be a state sales tax or FICA & FUTA taxes.

Example: The sales tax in (most of) my state of Virginia is 5.3% and it is the same for everyone in Virginia. If both you and Bill Gates (former Microsoft CEO and a billionaire) were to go to the local toy store and buy a bobblehead doll for $8.95, both you and he would pay sales tax on it of ($8.95 × 5.3%) = 47 cents. In fact, anyone (from the richest to the poorest) who bought that same $8.95 bobblehead would pay the same sales tax because it is a "flat" tax on everyone.

Progressive tax

A progressive tax will not stay the same for everyone. The percentage rate a person pays will increase along with their income. Federal income taxes are an example of a progressive tax.

More specific types of taxes

All taxes will either fall into the "flat" or "progressive" tax concept. Let's get into some more specific types of taxes.

FICA & FUTA Taxes

FICA stands for Federal Insurance Contributions Act. This is the Social Security tax (that was mentioned briefly in the prologue). It is also sometimes referred to as OASDI or Old Age, Survivor, and Disability Insurance. This is the tax that pays for retirees to receive Social Security benefits. It also pays an income for people who have been deemed by Social Security Disability Determination Services to be disabled and unable to work. Lastly, it helps pay for Medicare which is a government social insurance program that provides health insurance to those over age 65. It's paid by both you and your employer.

Unless you make well over $100,000 per year, FICA taxes are currently 6.2% of your total wages. Medicare taxes are an additional 1.45% of total wages.

FUTA stands for Federal Unemployment Tax Act and it is actually paid entirely by your employer. These taxes go to a fund that pays benefits to people who are unemployed. Today, it's generally a little over $430 per person, but again, this is only paid by employers.

Capital gains tax

When you invest in an asset, and later sell that asset for a profit, you will likely incur a capital gains tax. Note that you have to actually sell the asset to incur the tax. Just holding onto an asset while it goes up in value doesn't incur the tax. The tax is generally higher if you only held the asset for less than a year. Long-term assets are ones that you hold for longer than a year. When you sell these for a profit, then the capital gains tax is typically lower (perhaps even zero). The actual rates for short-term capital gains and long-term capital gains vary based on your income.

Federal income tax

The federal income tax is a tax on your income. It is a progressive tax, mentioned above and uses different income tax margins to determine your income tax liability. Your marginal tax is the tax you pay on the next $1 of income. The idea is to tax low-income earners less than high-income earners. Again, this is over-simplified, but Democrats tend to support marginal tax rates as fair, while Republicans believe that this may be a disincentive to work hard (and thus a detriment to the overall economy). While the dollar amounts taxed at different rates are typically adjusted for inflation each year, the tax rates themselves do not change that often. However, the overall tax rates were lowered (by Republican legislation – the Tax Cuts and Jobs Act) at the end of 2017 for the income that you will earn in 2018. For a single taxpayer, they are:

Taxable Income	Marginal Tax Rate
$0 - $9,525	10%
$9,525 - $38,700	12%
$38,700 - $82,500	22%
$82,500 - $157,500	24%
$157,500 - $200,000	32%
$200,000 - $500,000	35%
> $500,000	37%

Let's discuss an example of how marginal tax brackets work. Assume you have income of $38,700. Your income tax calculation would be $4,453.50 (but you should round off the cents).

- $9,525 would be taxed at 10% = $952.50
- $29,175 would be taxed at 12% = $3,501
- $952.50 + $3,501 = $4,454

Let's further assume that you get a $500 raise. Your first $9,525 is still taxed at 10% and the next $29,175 is still taxed at 12%. Only the $500 raise is taxed at 22%. Thus, your new tax liability is $4,564.

- $4,454 + ($500 × 22%) = $4,564

NOTE: *While this is your income tax calculation, it is not going to be your income tax liability, or what you "owe" in taxes. What you "owe" is likely to be less than this because of deductions and credits. We will discuss those shortly.*

What is tax withholding?

Many recent graduates are somewhat confused by the concept of tax withholding. You may notice that your employer "withholds" money from every paycheck and sends it directly to the IRS to cover your income tax liability. This is required by your employer so that the government regularly receives funds throughout the year rather than all in one lump sum at the end of the year. It is also done because the government knows there are a lot of people who would spend this money if they had it, and would not have funds available to meet their year-end tax liability if they hadn't "forced" the funding via withholding.

The amount you have withheld is not necessarily what you "owe" in taxes. Ideally, you would like to withhold just enough to meet your tax liability, but most of us either withhold too little (and owe taxes at the end of the year) or withhold too much (and receive a tax refund check).

NOTE: *Every year, the taxes you owe are due at or around April 15th of the following year. You should notice that after December 31st, you begin receiving tax documents from your employer, bank, brokerage, lenders, etc. Be sure to keep these documents and use them to file your taxes before "Tax Day".*

Calculating your income tax liability

To calculate your income tax liability, follow these six steps:

1. First calculate your *Total Income*.

2. Then subtract items that might be excludable from that income (*Adjusted Gross Income*).
3. Then apply any deductions and exemptions that are applicable to you (*Taxable Income*).
4. Then calculate the tax due using the marginal tax tables (above).
5. Finally, apply any *tax credits* you may enjoy.
6. From this, you now know if you owe taxes or if you have paid too much and are due a *refund*.

Trying to minimize taxes

The best way to minimize taxes is not to make any money; however, it is very difficult to get ahead and be financially successful if you have no income. Therefore, the second-best way is to try to have all of the *adjustments, deductions, and credits* you can to lower your overall tax liability. Then be sure your income tax preparer knows about them. Let's discuss some popular options for recent graduates:

Adjustments to gross income using retirement plan savings

I've devoted an entire chapter to retirement plans (chapter twelve). Retirement plans are not only a great way to plan for your financial independence; they are also a great way to lower your income tax liability, as some retirement plans allow you to lower your taxable income this year by every $1 that you save into them.

Example: Let's go back to the marginal tax bracket example that we use earlier (the one where you made $38,700 and then received a $500 raise – and owed $4,564 in taxes). If you had saved $200 of your $500 raise into a

BECAUSE NO ONE IS GOING TO TAKE CARE OF YOU

qualified retirement plan, this would have lowered your tax liability by $44 to just $4,520 (rather than $4,564). This is a win/win! You get retirement savings (which is awesome) and you get a lower tax liability today (which is also awesome).

Here is a great habit. Whenever you get a raise, increase your retirement savings contribution at the same time. It's generally difficult for most people to make "savings sacrifices" from income they already enjoy. But you won't miss the feeling of receiving money that you never had! For instance, if you are fortunate enough to receive an actual $500 per year raise, it is a tremendously smart financial move to concurrently increase the amount you regularly save into your qualified retirement plan by at least $200. With the raise (and the increased savings) you will still enjoy $300 in increased income, you will lower your overall tax liability, and you will be saving for your future financial success (this is a win/win/win).

Student loan interest

Another adjustment that can lower your taxable income is qualified student loan interest if you are currently repaying a student loan. There are a few stipulations, but your tax accountant/income tax preparer will discuss these with you to be sure that you qualify.

NOTE: *America almost lost this deduction in the new tax bill. Fortunately, for those who qualify, a sufficient number of higher education leaders and students fought for you to keep it. However, the primary reasoning that Washington lawmakers used to try to get it removed was that it was "too complicated and many qualifying*

68

taxpayers failed to use it". Please don't let this hard-earned victory go to waste by failing to claim your deduction!

The new "standard" deduction

The Tax Cuts and Jobs Act passed at the end of 2017 has increased the amount of the standard deduction to $12,000 for individual taxpayers. This means that any American taxpayer is able to subtract this "standard" deduction of $12,000 from his/her income before calculating their tax liability in 2018. Going forward, this amount is likely to increase each year to adjust for inflation.

You may still choose to "itemize" your deductions rather than take the "standard" deduction, but the increased amount of the standard deduction has likely decreased the number of taxpayers who would benefit from itemizing. This could be a good thing – in that it may make your taxes significantly easier to calculate, but be sure to consult your tax advisor to be sure.

NOTE: Fortunately, you do not need to itemize your deductions to take the student loan interest deduction mentioned earlier. It is an "above-the-line" deduction for those who qualify.

Tax credits

A tax credit is a dollar for dollar reduction in the tax liability you owe. They are kind of a big deal if you can get one. One tax credit in which many recent graduates might qualify is an education credit. This credit can help offset the costs of education. A second popular tax credit for young people (with young people of their own) is the child tax credit. If you have a child, then this credit may offer you a substantial reduction in your tax liability – and a portion of it may even be refundable to you, even if you do not owe taxes.

Don't leave any money on the table

The items listed in this chapter are just a few of the possible items that could help you reduce your income tax liability. While these may be popular options for a recent graduate, there are many more! If you think you have any opportunity to lower your tax liability, I suggest that you get a tax professional to help you with your income tax preparation. I'm pretty comfortable with tax filing, and I don't do mine without help. I use tax preparation software to be sure that I've found every single adjustment, deduction, and credit that I'm entitled to receive. I don't mind paying my fair share, but I don't want to pay one cent more!

In deciding on a tax accountant, if you have a friend or family member who can help you, then they may be your best bet. You want someone whom you trust. If you don't have this option, here are some tips for selecting a tax accountant:

- Be sure to check your preparer's qualifications. All paid tax return preparers have a Preparer Tax Identification Number (PTIN). In addition to making sure they have a PTIN, ask if the preparer is affiliated with a professional organization and attends continuing education classes.
- Run a check on your preparer. See if anything comes up when you search his/her name. Check with the Better Business Bureau. If they are a Certified Public Accountant (CPA) then check the website for your

state's board of accountancy. If they are an attorney, then check your state's bar association.

- Try to avoid preparers who base their fee on the percentage of your refund or those who claim they can get you a larger refund than other preparers. This is a red flag. Also, if your preparer suggests that any portion of your refund go to them – find another preparer. You want your refund to go to you only!

- Be sure you collect every single record, statement, and receipt before having your taxes done. Your preparer should look at your documents and ask you questions. If they don't – red flag!

- Get someone you like and deem professional. They should be available if you have issues and/or questions and they should be sure you understand everything before they ask you to sign off on your forms.

- You may not feel like you know much about taxes, but you know enough. Be sure to look over everything on your forms before signing. If there is a question – ask! It's okay to look ignorant. Once you've given the okay, note that your tax preparer should sign them too and give you a copy...

♦ † ♦

♦ CHAPTER SEVEN ♦

RISK PROTECTION

I'm going to get a little hateful for just a moment. When it comes to personal finance, I don't like "rules of thumb". I believe that financial planning is too complicated and too specific to each individual for a "rule of thumb" to be helpful. There are some financial talking heads on television who have a rule of thumb for this and that. When I see them, I change the channel. They kind of upset me. Now, that being said, when it comes to managing risks, I'm going to give you a rule of thumb.

Frequency & severity

Take several moments and think through the risks you have in your life. You may want to write them down as there are a lot. Here are just a few to get you started:

- The risk that there is an earthquake
- The risk that you get into a fender bender

- The risk of not being able to work for a short while
- The risk that you get into a major auto accident
- The risk that you won't be able to work for a long while
- The risk that a thief steals your wallet
- The risk to others if you die
- The risk that you require hospital treatment

Now – I'd like you to go back over your risk-list and classify each risk on two criteria: the frequency at which they are likely to occur and the financial severity of the impact.

Example: Where I live in Roanoke, Virginia, the frequency of earthquakes is very low. If we ever had an earthquake, I'm betting it would be a small one that no one would feel, so the severity for me is also low. However, if I lived in California, I would likely have labeled this differently.

Once you have classified your risks, then there are several strategies for managing them:

1. *Retention* – plan to pay the cost if the loss occurs
2. *Avoidance* – don't expose yourself to the risk
3. *Reduction* – take some action to lower the frequency and/or severity of the risk
4. *Transfer* – purchase insurance and pass the risk to the insurer

A general rule of thumb when it comes to managing risks is to:

- *Retain* the low-frequency/low severity-risks

- *Transfer* the low-frequency/high-severity risks
- *Reduce* the high-frequency/low severity risk
- *Avoid* the high-frequency/high-severity risks

That being said, I'm going to recommend that you consult with your financial advisor about everything you just did. I don't know if I mentioned it, but I'm not a big fan of rules of thumb. In addition, for some of these strategies, you may need to get really creative for them to work. Others may not work at all. For instance, if where you live, your frequency of earthquakes is high, and the severity of them is also high – then how can you avoid them? I guess you would need to move – which may or may not be plausible…

Insurance

I do, however, want to share with you some of the risk transfer options that you have available to you. Transferring risk typically means purchasing insurance. When you purchase insurance, you will contract with an insurer to determine the benefits that they will pay if the risk occurs. In addition, you will want to be clear on the rules the insurer uses to determine whether or not the risk occurred. In some cases (life insurance for example) the rules are pretty clear, but in other cases like "disability insurance" the qualifications can be much more complicated. Lastly, you will need to determine the cost (or premium payments needed) for this protection.

Several different types of insurance are provided to you by the government. The "premiums" for this protection are paid by your tax dollars. Other types of insurance may be included in the benefits package offered by your employer. In my experience, a lot of people have benefits from their employer that they don't even know about. If you can't find a list of your employer-provided benefits on-line, then check the packet of documents you were likely provided when you were hired. If you can't find that, then ask your firm's human resources representative about the company-sponsored insurance benefits for which you may be eligible.

Health insurance

As you re-educate yourself on your employer-provided benefits, hopefully you will find that you are covered or have access to coverage from a group healthcare plan. One of the biggest financial problems facing Americans today is the cost of healthcare, and it is only getting worse. Therefore, it is of the utmost importance that you have some protection against the potentially debilitating costs of healthcare.

Oftentimes, employers are able to provide you with significant cost savings with a group health insurance plan. If your employer offers coverage (and you currently have none) then it is vital that you sign up for this protection as soon as possible. It is also terribly important that even if you have the best healthcare plan in the universe, that you still focus on prevention by staying healthy. Keep your weight under control by eating a balanced diet and getting regular exercise. Find time for rest and relaxation. Avoid smoking and the over-use of alcohol. And drive carefully!

NOTE: *Even if you do everything in your power to prevent healthcare problems – you still need coverage whether it is provided by your employer or not. If you need to obtain an individual healthcare policy, check out* Healthcare.gov.

There are several different types of health insurance plans, and your employer may offer you several options. When deciding on the type of health insurance policy that may make the most financial sense for you, consider your health needs. As a young person, you might not need the same level of protection as someone your parents' age. However, what is your family history of health problems? Are your parents and grandparents healthy or do they have some pretty serious ailments? Genetics may play a big role in the level of coverage you need. In addition, think through other aspects of your life. Are you a chain-smoking couch potato who occasionally enjoys cliff jumping? Or are you an avid marathoner who eats 7 servings of vegetables a day and gets 8-hours of sleep every night?

Use your health needs analysis to determine the level of health coverage that makes the most sense for you and enroll in it. There are currently three popular options when it comes to health coverage:

- *Preferred Provider Organizations (PPOs)* are typically the most expensive option but arguably provide you with the most flexible and comprehensive coverage.
- *Health Maintenance Organizations (HMOs)* are generally less expensive than PPOs but will require you to get a "referral" from your Primary Care Physician (PCP) before you can see any other physicians – and the list of physician options may be relatively limited.
- *High-Deductible Health Plans (HDHPs)* are relatively new but may make financial sense for relatively healthy young people. They are usually

used in conjunction with a Health Savings Account (HSA).

High-Deductible Health Plans (HDHPs) generally have lower premiums and higher deductibles than other types of healthcare coverage. It just makes sense that premiums would be lower if you carry a higher deductible. A deductible is the amount you have to pay before the insurance company will step up and cover any costs. The IRS currently defines a HDHP as any plan with a deductible of at least $1,350 for an individual.

Example: Assume you have a $1,350 deductible on your HDHP, and you require healthcare that costs $1,351. You will be required to pay $1,350 since that is your deductible. The insurance company will then step in to pay the final $1. However, after the deductible is met, the insurance company will pay for any additional costs (generally no matter how high) for the remainder of the plan year. If you are comfortable with doing so, I'm a proponent of carrying a high deductible on healthcare coverage assuming 1) you are healthy and do not frequently need healthcare and 2) you have a sufficiently large emergency fund to meet the deductible.

In a sense, you are "retaining" a portion of the risk, and "transferring" the remainder. Since you are retaining some of the risk, then transferring the rest doesn't cost you as much. Unfortunately, without a sufficiently large emergency fund, this strategy may not be wise. Therefore, in order to motivate you to retain a sufficiently large emergency fund, the HDHP is frequently accompanied by the option to save a portion of your paycheck regularly into a Health Savings Account (HSA).

These savings vehicles are pretty cool in that you can grow your HSA tax-free. If you don't use it, you can roll it over into the next year. In fact, if you never use your HSA savings while you are young, you could potentially use your HSA to save thousands of dollars to help fund your healthcare needs in retirement – all tax free. Again, I wonder if these plans wouldn't make financial sense for many recent graduates.

NOTE: *If I would have had access to these plans when I was in my twenties, I would have been all over them... and I believe I would be in even better financial shape today because of it*

Disability insurance

Your ability to work and earn an income over the course of your lifetime is one of your most precious commodities. Without this ability, your chances of financial success are severely diminished and some studies estimate that as many as one in three of us will become disabled for three months or more during our lifetimes. Disability insurance protects you against losing this ability to work. Many of us can handle minor disabilities with personal and sick leave from our jobs. However, more severe disabilities may require either short-term or long-term disability insurance. A short-term disability policy typically provides you income in the event that you cannot work for up to two years (but the average policy only pays for 6 months). If you are still unable to work after this period, then a long-term policy usually kicks in and pays until age 65.

In order to qualify for your own individual short-term and long-term policies, you will typically have to show a history of earning an income. Individual policies can usually provide you with up to 60% of your current income in the event you are disabled. The policy will dictate exactly what is and what isn't considered a disability. If the policy has a liberal definition of disability, then it is likely to have higher premiums than a policy with a strict definition of disability.

While I think they are a good idea, I know very few people with individual disability policies. Many people have disability coverage through their employer. This is usually sufficient for their needs and typically less expensive than an individual policy, but a potential reason for obtaining your own individual coverage is that once you have it, you can keep it. You will lose your group coverage at your job if you leave that job.

The government also provides Social Security Disability Insurance (SSDI). Qualifying for SSDI is fairly easy, but obtaining it is extremely difficult. SSDI has a strict "any employment" definition to disability that makes it difficult to meet the requirements to receive the benefits.

Life insurance

It is extremely simple to calculate the "frequency vs. severity" numbers for the risk that you will die. The frequency is "one" and the financial impact to you is "zero". However, life insurance isn't for us, it is for those who depend on us. If no one depends on you, then you probably don't have a need for life insurance. If you have a spouse and children who need you to contribute financially to their needs, then life insurance may become a good way to protect them. If you die while a life insurance policy is in force, then the agreed upon death benefit is paid in cash – tax-free to your beneficiary. However, you must pay the stated premiums on the policy or the policy may lapse. Premiums will get higher as you get older since the chances of you passing away increases as you age. In addition, premiums will be higher if you are not healthy and they will be significantly higher if you are a smoker. The insurance company will likely put you through the underwriting process (that will likely include a physical exam) to determine your overall health before issuing you a policy. When you apply for life insurance (or any type of insurance for that matter) – read every word of your policy and ask questions if anything is unclear.

The question then becomes, is that need permanent or temporary. If the need is permanent, then permanent (cash value) insurance is likely the best fit. However, if the need is only temporary, then term insurance might be a better suited product.

Permanent life insurance

In a much oversimplified description, for a permanent insurance (or cash value) policy, you are going to pay more premium into the policy than is really required to meet the insurance company's cost while you are younger. The insurer will take out their costs (and some profit) and the extra that you paid in will remain (and hopefully grow). The cool thing about the money that remains in the policy is that it grows tax-deferred, and these dollars can help you meet the higher costs that the insurance company incurs for protecting you as you get older. If enough money is paid in, then the insurer will promise to pay out the death benefit of the policy no matter when you die (today up to any age).

NOTE: Permanent policies have many options when it comes to what "investment" your extra dollars are placed into. Speak with your insurance agent about what might make sense for you.

At your age, I can't really imagine that you would have much in the way of a permanent need for life insurance. These policies are good fits for those with estate planning and business needs. However, you may have a desire to meet your final expenses (funeral, etc.) This is likely a permanent need. Again, speak with your insurance agent or financial advisor about what might make sense.

Term insurance

Term insurance on the other hand is "pure" insurance. You pay the cost that the insurance company incurs (and some profit) for the period that you require a death benefit. The period can be set by you. It can be 10, 20, or even 30 years. Typically, the longer the term, the higher the premiums. This is because the chances of you dying over the next 30 years are much greater than the chances of you dying over the next 10 years... The insurance company needs to account for that fact.

NOTE: A good use of term insurance might be to pay for your child's college education. Let's assume that you have a 4-year old daughter. If you want to be sure that you pay for her college, even if you pass away, you might purchase a 20-year term policy with enough death benefit to cover her college tuition. The 20-year protection will end at about the same time she graduates from college.

Life insurance is another benefit that many employers will provide. Your employer's life insurance benefits can vary widely. However, I often see employer benefits equal to one year's salary, or $50,000. These just seem to be two popular options. Again, you most likely lose these life insurance benefits if you leave your job.

Long-term care insurance

Long-term care insurance isn't for you (yet). I bring it up here because you may want to talk to your parents about their need for this protection. A long-term care stay (in a nursing home or hospice) can be terribly expensive. The national average is approximately $81,000 per year. The average stay is relatively short, but it is possible to require long-term care for many years. Would you be able to help your parents with this expense if they required it?

If your parents are loaded and can afford the expense – then that is great. However, if they can't then they should think about speaking with a financial advisor regarding their options. There is "long-term care insurance" but the premiums for this coverage have risen significantly in recent years. Regardless, long-term care insurance may still be the best way to protect against this expense.

Note that your parents may tell you that long-term care is covered by Medicare. Many people think this, but this thinking is mostly wrong. Medicare may pay for a few weeks' worth of long-term care, but that is it. It is true that they may be covered by Medicaid, but only after they have basically gone bankrupt – and then only at Medicaid sponsored facilities.

Protecting your financial success

Insurance is not a popular topic. In fact, in business education, it is the pinnacle example often used when marketing professors discuss "unsought products". However, it would be terrible to have a potentially insurable expense ruin all of your hard work. It is important to regularly access your protection needs (frequency × severity) and maintain adequate insurance to address any needs that may pop up. Note that two more important insurance tools (homeowner's insurance and automobile insurance) will be covered in chapter ten.

◆ † ◆

CHAPTER EIGHT

USING A CREDIT CARD RESPONSIBLY

Let's talk for a moment about a drug – specifically, a painkiller. A painkiller can be great! It can take an aspect of your everyday life (pain) and help you with it. It can help you get through the day and even make you generally happier. However, painkillers can also ruin your life. If you don't use painkillers responsibly, you could become addicted. You NEED the painkillers. You can't get through a day without them. Are you happier because of them? No! You are miserable! In fact, if you don't do something to break yourself of the cycle, they can destroy you.

Substitute "credit cards" for "painkillers" and everything in the above paragraph is still true. I love credit cards for what they can do for people and I despise credit cards for what they can do for people. If you are going to use credit, you MUST do it responsibly. I'm going to go into some depth regarding the features and strategies of credit cards, but my advice is extremely simple. <u>Do not charge more</u>

<u>than you can pay off each month</u>. If you can't stick to this strategy, I'm going to go ahead and beg you not to get one. Please!!! Let me explain why I'm so passionate about this topic.

Consumer credit

Consumer credit (credit cards, automobile loans, student loans, home equity loans, etc.) allow you to receive goods, services, and even cash now as long as you arrange to pay it back later. You can use consumer credit responsibly as long as you stick to your schedule when it comes to paying it back. Unfortunately, too many Americans use consumer credit to get something they want now with little or no regard as to the budgeting needed to pay off the debt. When this process persists, it generally results in bankruptcy.

NOTE: *Fortunately, the number of bankruptcies has been on the decline. In the United States in 2014 (when this book was first published), there were 1.4 million bankruptcies. In 2016, there were less than 800,000.*

Some egregiously irresponsible consumers have no plan to get out of the consumer debt they accumulate. They know they will eventually file bankruptcy but plan to enjoy life as much as possible until that day comes. This attitude is detestable. But unlike those who plan bankruptcy, many more consumers who eventually end up filing for bankruptcy started off innocently enough. There was no ill intent. Their path to bankruptcy started by simply carrying a small balance on their credit card. It didn't seem like that big of a deal. Since it worked so well the first time, they decided to buy something else that they couldn't quite afford. No big deal... just put it on the card...

I call this activity "circling the drain". Before long, many will max out one card and then have to get another... and another... and so on... Once it starts, it's really hard for many people to stop. After a few years of circling the drain, it becomes evident that there is no way out – except to throw up their hands and declare bankruptcy. I wouldn't call this detestable, but I would call it irresponsible. These filers are basically telling the financial community that they cannot responsibly handle credit. They are like a small child finding a cookie jar. One cookie is pretty tasty, so may as well have one more. Before long, the child with no capability of restraint, or cognition of consequences, has eaten so many cookies that they throw up all over the kitchen. Then a responsible adult has to come in and clean it up. Bankruptcy filings are not free. Everyone is likely paying higher fees and interest because of this irresponsible behavior.

Ironically, even though the credit abuser's actions are like that of a child, older Americans will likely be able to get away with this type of irresponsible behavior better than you will. Do you remember why? Because you are going to help take care of them. No one is going to take care of you.

I know this sounds harsh. I just want to make it very clear that if you use credit, it is really important that you use it wisely. There isn't much I can think of that would be worse for your chances of financial success than the irresponsible use of credit.

Do you need a credit card yet?

Arc you sure you even really need a credit card? I've

stated that you need a bank account, but I will not state the same thing about a credit card. You can do fine without one. If you have never had a credit card, you won't miss what you've never had. For a lot of consumers, getting a credit card is to become almost instantly addicted to it. Why have the addiction? In a way, don't you have greater freedom without it?

When I tell some students this, they ask me how they will build a credit history without a credit card. "Isn't a credit history important?" Yes it is – but the responsible payment of any debt builds your credit history (student loans for example). And for too many young people, when they get a credit card, they only do damage to their credit score. Miss a payment or two and your credit score will plummet. Building it back takes serious time too. You want a credit card to help build a strong credit history, but unless you are positive you can be 100% responsible, you will only hurt your credit score, with repercussions that can last for years.

In addition, students often tell me they need a credit card because of how convenient the credit card makes purchases. I agree, it is convenient, but isn't a prepaid card or a debit card just as convenient?

Debit vs credit

Debit cards are generally issued to you when you open up your bank account. In many ways, they work exactly like a credit card. They are accepted at most establishments which can make purchases convenient. They also provide the same record-keeping ease that credit cards provide (a monthly consolidated statement). I used to advise others that credit cards were safer because of their fraud protection features, but this is not the case anymore. It depends on the bank where you get your debit card, but most have fraud protection very similar to that of a credit card. Some even have your picture on it! As you research banks (chapter four), be sure to ask about the features of the bank's debit card.

The key difference between a debt and a credit card is that when you "charge" something on your debit card, you don't pay later as you would with a credit card. The money comes out of your account right then. Therefore, you have to have sufficient funds in your account to meet the needs of the transaction. Some banks will actually text or email you when your account is getting low to help you keep this from happening. But it is terribly important that you do not overcharge your debit card – or your bank is likely to get upset.

Obtaining your first credit card

Okay, so my efforts to persuade you to go without a credit card have fallen on deaf ears... To be clear, I'm not against your getting a credit card, I just worry about you. Someone else who is likely to worry about you is your mom and dad. I know you probably want to be independent (a successful trait), but it might be a good idea to have one of these loved ones (or some other loved one) with you when you apply for your first card. If they are willing, they can co-sign your credit application. By co-signing, they are stating that if you act irresponsibly, they will step up and meet your obligations. If your parents have a strong credit history, your bank is really going to be comforted by this and likely give you better terms on your card than you could get otherwise. But, be sure you and your mom, dad, sibling (whoever) know what you are getting into, and are comfortable with the arrangement. If a loved one understands the risks and is still willing to help you, in my opinion, you should accept it. Having a co-signed card does build a credit history for you.

A secured card

If this isn't an option, then another option for you might be something known as a "secured credit card" which may be more prominent at credit unions. I'm a fan of this strategy as well, because you can only get into so much trouble before the credit union steps in and prevents you from getting into any more. With a secured card, you get a credit limit that is equal to a deposit you make with your credit union. For instance, if you deposit $500, then the credit card you receive has a $500 limit (i.e. you won't be allowed to charge more than $500 on it). Your deposit "secures" the card compared to most cards which are "unsecured". You might think that these cards would have good terms, but in my experience, they aren't that great. However, if you prove to the credit union (and yourself) that you can handle the secured card, then the credit union is likely going to be willing to issue you an unsecured card within a year or two... You may also want to ask your credit union if their secured card reports to the credit rating agencies to build your credit history. They should – but be sure.

A "starter/student/college" or retailer card

Other than these options, if you are a student or recent graduate, and you haven't done anything that would be a red flag to a credit card company, you might find that you are able to obtain an unsecured credit card on your own. You typically don't have to demonstrate much income to obtain a card with a designation like "starter, college, or student". You may also be able to obtain a card from a retailer. Store cards sometimes provide you with significant discounts if you use them in that store. However, starter cards and store cards typically have terribly high interest rates and very little in the way of grace periods (the time between new charges and your due date). As long as you never charge more than you can pay off each month – you should be okay.

But the first time you decide to carry a balance forward to the next month; you are taking your first circle of the drain, and I'm afraid you won't be able to stop. I know it will probably seem okay and not that big of a deal… Just this once… right?

You might be right. I kind of doubt it, but maybe you will pay it off and be fine. Regardless, while you carry a credit card balance, you are not moving in the right financial direction. There is almost nothing you can do (that makes financial sense) to move toward financial independence if you carry a credit card balance. Sometimes, people with thousands of dollars of credit card debt ask me what investments I'd recommend for them… My response is: "Let me ask you – what is the interest rate on your credit card?" Let's assume it's about 19%. "Let me ask you something else – what can I invest you in that guarantees you a 19% return on your investment?" The answer is nothing… If you carry credit card debt, no other financial move makes more sense than paying off that debt. There is no individual investment that you can save $1 into that will do more for you than using that $1 to pay off your credit card (with one exception – see chapter twelve).

Let's flip sides for a moment and assume you don't have any credit card debt. If you have $1 to invest, you have the opportunity to use your $1 to buy stock in a credit card company. You can then reap the benefits of those who don't use credit responsibly. In a way, they are paying interest to you. Be a lender not a borrower!

The minimum payment

I'd like to make one last point on carrying a credit card balance. A lot of consumers are fooled by the "minimum payment" that their credit card requires. The minimum payment is the payment that you must make each month to remain in "good standing", but it is often very low in relation to the balance. Making only the minimum payment is a recipe for financial disaster.

Assume that you have a $1,000 balance on your credit card, the interest rate on your card is 16% (which is better than mine...) and your minimum required payment is $15 per month. How many months do you think it will take you to pay off this $1,000 debt (assuming you don't charge anything else)? Would you guess maybe 60 months (5 years)? After 5 years of making the minimum payment, you still owe $848 on the original $1,000 debt. For this example, you will finally pay off your debt after 166 months (over 14 years). You will pay a total of $2,490 for your $1,000 charge. How could someone get ahead financially, making these kinds of decisions?! Like I said, making only the minimum payment starts you on your path to circling the drain. Do not charge more than you can pay off each month.

Are there any positives to credit cards?

It sounds like I have a strong dislike for credit cards, doesn't it? I actually don't. I dislike that credit cards can tempt people into using them irresponsibly. Used responsibly; however, credit cards have several positive attributes. Several of these attributes, I've already discussed, because they are shared with debit cards, but let's go into a little greater detail.

Consolidated statements

The ease of record-keeping is one very positive quality associated with credit cards. When budgeting, credit card statements are a fantastic way to keep an eye on your spending habits.

Protection

I feel credit cards provide several different types of protection. One way they protect you is that they provide you the opportunity to carry less cash. This can make you less vulnerable to muggings. Many muggers will pick their targets by watching for someone to "flash some cash". The mugger has little interest in your card. They know you will just call the credit card company and cancel it – so why bother?

Credit card companies have also become masters of dealing with stolen cards and fraud. I've actually had my credit card number stolen twice (once by a waitress and once by a skimmer at a gas station). The credit card company dealt with both these incidents so efficiently, that it was basically a non-event for me. Both times, they recognized the fraudulent activity, contacted me about it, cancelled the card, and sent me a new card within 2 days.

NOTE: *Even though the process of having my credit card number stolen was painless, now I do try to keep a close eye on my card whenever I hand it over to someone… And I quit using that gas station.*

Time value of money

One of the features of credit cards is that you buy now and pay later. In finance, "paying later" is almost always a good thing because it means you get to keep your money (and possibly earn interest on it) longer. By using a credit card, and paying it off each month, you get to delay the actual removing of the funds from your account by a little longer.

Example: Let's assume that your checking account earns 1.2% per year (this is currently laughably high – but I'm just trying to make a point here). This means that your account earns .1% each month. Let's also assume that you make a $10,000 purchase on your credit card on May 1st, and your credit card due date isn't until June 1st (at which time you will pay it off). This means that the $10,000 gets to remain in your account for one whole month and is able to earn interest ($10,000 × .1%) of $10. By delaying the payment, you earned $10 that you would not have earned if the $10,000 had come out of your account on the day you made the purchase.

NOTE: *Do you see how this wouldn't work with a debit card? With a debit card, the funds are removed when you make the purchase.*

If you don't pay the card off each month, the interest you get charged is significantly higher than any interest you might earn (thus completely ruining the "positive" effect of it).

Rewards

Some credit cards offer "rewards". A reward is basically an incentive for you to use the card. The rewards could be "miles" for frequent flyers, hotel rewards, gift cards, or (my favorite) cash. You qualify for these rewards by making charges on your card. Oftentimes, these rewards range from 1% to 5% of purchases. There are numerous types of rewards and the choice among the cards can become daunting, but I've actually seen some really helpful websites that will aid you in choosing the right rewards card for you. If you are considering a new credit card, you may want to check out www.creditkarma.com and/or www.creditcards.com.

Example: For my particular rewards card, this quarter, for every $1 that I spend at Lowes, I get 5 cents back in rewards (I only get 1% back for every other purchase). So, let's say I put $1,000 of purchases from Lowes on my card this quarter. Next, I can go to my card's website, fill out a couple of blanks, and my credit card company will mail me either a check for cash or a gift card for ($1,000 × 5%) = $50. Not too bad…

NOTE: There is a risk worth mentioning here. When some consumers get their rewards card, it causes them to overspend, because they keep thinking about all the cash they are going to get back. This is obviously kind of dumb, but I'll be honest, I had some of these silly thoughts too when I first got my card… Just be careful.

Building a credit history

You may not need a credit card to build a strong financial history, but if you use them responsibly, they can positively influence your credit score. With a strong credit score, you will qualify for loans at the best rates (mortgages, auto loans, lines-of-credit, etc.). Something to consider, however, is that if you have too much credit, it actually lowers your credit score. Even if you use credit responsibly, don't apply for cards that you don't really need. A popular place to get into trouble here is with too many store credit cards. Be aware that if you are tempted to apply for a store's credit card to obtain a discount at that store; you may enjoy the discount, but you may also be lowering your credit score. Lastly, it's also best to not make a habit of frequently switching from one card to another. Reviewers of your credit report like to see stability. Pick a card that meets your needs and stick to it for the long run if you can.

But do you know the absolute best thing you can do to improve your credit score? <u>Do not charge more than you can pay off each month</u>.

◆ † ◆

♦ CHAPTER NINE ♦

PAYING FOR & PAYING OFF HIGHER EDUCATION EXPENSES

It is my hope that you can skip this chapter entirely. It is my hope that you have completed all of the higher education that you ever intend to complete and that you have no student debt to show for it. However, if this is not the case, you still may be able to skip half of this chapter. As the title of this book suggests, the contents are for the "recent graduate" be that a graduation from high school, college, or graduate school. However, as you head out on your own for the first time, depending on your most recent graduation, you may be in very different financial shape from other readers. Specifically, college graduates tend to have increased earnings potential but much more debt than do high school graduates. Let's first assume that you are a high school graduate and wonder if you might like to one day explore the opportunity of increasing your earnings potential by going to college…

Thinking about going to college one day?

As a college educator, you might guess that I have a very high opinion of the benefits of a college education. Speaking personally, I know that I graduated from college a very different (and arguably) better person than I was going in. A college education provided me with a confidence in myself that I don't think I would have obtained otherwise. I see the same changes in my students today. The students I have as seniors are generally very different people than they were as freshman. They not only mature over the four years, they gain self-esteem. They also gain focus. Many freshmen truly believe they are interested in some particular subject only to find that their true passion lies elsewhere. College provides much more than just "book-learning". But it is definitely not for everyone.

Are you sure college is going to help you?

Again, I think a college education is great, but for the purposes of this writing, I want to focus solely on the "financial" reasons for attending college. While college is awesome, it is also ridiculously expensive, and the costs are rising on average about 7% per year. Even after you write the check for your tuition and fees, there are other notable expenses – room and board, textbooks, notebooks, laptops, software, etc. The "average" college graduate owes $37,000 in student loans the day after commencement and this number is growing every year. Therefore - the above-mentioned benefits aside – you must ask yourself if college would truly benefit you financially.

According to the National Center for Education Statistics, the mean earnings for college graduates is almost $17,000 more per year than that of high school graduates. Over a lifetime of working, this difference can amount to hundreds of thousands of dollars. In addition, college graduates may enjoy more promotion opportunities and upward mobility than high school graduates. However, not every major enjoys these same financial benefits. Do you believe you would be one of them?

For instance, some college students will return home to work in the family business. Is college really necessary for these students if they are already guaranteed the job (and have a family member to train them)? Wouldn't they make the same amount of money regardless? In addition, some college students major in disciplines like leisure studies, animal science or sociology and then become electricians, financial advisors, or HVAC professionals. Did college really help prepare them in any way for this work?

From a purely financial perspective, it doesn't make sense to go through the ordeal of paying for college if it is not going to benefit you in your chosen profession or career plan. Yes – college can be a great time! But so is Disneyworld and even at the outrageous prices you pay there – it is still way less expensive than college.

What do you think about community college or a technical school?

Community colleges are two-year educations institutions that offer associate degrees and other certifications. They tend to focus on preparing students for a specific profession (perhaps dental hygiene, business administration, medical technology, or network administration). Technical schools are very similar. Generally, both options are much more affordable than traditional four-year institutions. The average tuition for community college is less than half that of a four-year institution (and even less than that if you remain in-state). In addition, if you have your heart set on attending a four-year institution, many community colleges have agreements in place that allow you to easily transfer your community college credits to a four-year institution after two years. By engaging in this strategy, you save a significant amount of money (over the first two years) and your diploma looks exactly the same as everyone else's who graduated from that four-year college.

If you have your heart set on going to a four-year institution

If you are certain that a college education makes sense for you, then your first step is to complete the Free Application for Federal Student Aid (FAFSA) form online at fafsa.gov. It is fairly straightforward, but if you have questions, the site can provide you with a lot of help. Then, consider the following:

- **Is someone else willing to help you pay for your college expenses?**

In some cases, your parents (or even other family members) may have been saving to help you pay for this expense. If they are willing, and it will not place a financial burden on them, then you may want to take them up on their help.

In addition, some employers may be willing to help you pay for your college courses if you can demonstrate how they will benefit from your newfound knowledge.

- **Do you have time (over five years) to save before you desire to go to college?**

If so, consider putting your college savings dollars into a Roth IRA (which will be discussed in chapter twelve). By saving into a retirement plan, you can grow your savings tax-deferred and you won't hurt your chances of qualifying for financial aid. In addition, the Roth IRA lets you easily withdraw funds to pay for college, and if you change your mind later about your desire to attend college, then you have some great retirement savings already built up.

- **Do you qualify for any scholarships or grants?**

This is free money! You don't have to pay back grants and scholarships but you will most likely have to do some research to see which ones you might be able to obtain. The grants and scholarships link on the website, www.studentaid.ed.gov is a good place to start.

Don't just apply for the big scholarships. The smaller ones are often much easier to obtain. If you have to write a paper or something – even better! Not many students will apply if it means they have to do some actual work which greatly increases your odds.

- **What student loans are you able to obtain?**

Generally, federal loans are preferable to private loans. They have lower interest rates and more flexible payment options. In addition, many federal student loans are "subsidized" which means that the government pays the interest on these loans while you are in school.

- **Check with your school's financial aid office. They can help you understand your options much better than anyone.**

I'm done with school; now how do I pay off these loans?

First off – congratulations! You did it! Now, let's get to work so that these loans don't ruin your life. The good news is that paying off your student loans is very simple. You need to earn an income, and live within your means. If you can consistently do these two things – you will be out from under this debt in no time.

Paying back your federal loans

The first step is to be sure you know the amount of debt that you have. The majority of loans made to most college students are federal loans which tend to be better deals than private loans. However, since many college students get new loans every semester, it is actually very easy to lose track. Unfortunately, the federal government will not be very understanding if you "forget" to pay them back. To be sure you are aware of all the debt you have incurred, check out the National Student Loan Data System at www.nslds.ed.gov. This is the Department of Education's central database for student aid and it should provide you with a list of all the federal loans that were made to you over your college career.

The standard repayment plan for federal loans is a fixed monthly payment that will retire your debt in ten years. If this payment is a complete impossibility for you given your current financial situation, then you do have some options. While I wouldn't advise this strategy unless you have no other recourse, you can choose to change your payment plan to some other plan with lower monthly payments; however, be aware that if you do this, you will be paying more in interest over the life of the loan.

NOTE: *My strong advice is to try to budget your spending in a way so that you can pay MORE than the standard payment. You would be amazed how much more quickly your loans disappear by paying more than required. To receive the biggest bang for your buck, dedicate your overpayment to the debt with the highest interest rate (this includes other debts like credit cards and private loans, as well).*

If you still have not found employment, and have no income, there is also the option to defer payments for up to three years or receive a temporary forbearance from paying on your student loans. If you cannot pay, it is imperative that you speak with the lender to obtain an official reprieve from making payments or you could find yourself in default. Check out the deferment and forbearance links on www.studentaid.ed.gov for more information.

A loophole for federal loans

While I would generally advise you to pay more than the "standard" payment plan for your federal loan repayment schedule, there are some exceptions to this rule.

- Are you planning to join the military?
- Are you a full-time teacher (especially in a low-income school district) or a librarian?
- Are you a cop?
- Are you a nurse or a doctor (especially in a remote region)?
- Do you work for the government or a non-profit?

- Are you planning to join the Peace Corps?

If any of these options are true for you, then you may qualify for federal student loan forgiveness. It is possible that if you make regular payments for ten years, then the remainder of your debt may be forgiven. In some circumstances, the loan forgiveness may be more immediate and/or substantial (military service, teachers in low-income areas, healthcare workers in remote locations, and Peace Corp volunteers). To help you understand the full ramifications of this strategy is beyond the scope of this writing. However, you can check out the loan forgiveness link on www.studentaid.ed.gov for more information if you believe you might qualify. In addition, strongly consider consulting with a financial advisor about this strategy. Structured properly, your potential out-of-pocket savings could be huge.

Paying back your private loans

Just like federal loans, you need to be sure you have accounted for all of your private loans. There is no on-line database that compiles private loans like the National Student Loan Data System does with federal loans, so you may want to contact your school's financial aid office if you think you may have missed any. Most private lenders do a pretty good job of keeping in contact with you, but if they don't – then contact them! They haven't forgotten about you and if you fail in your obligated payments, the bank will become upset.

NOTE: *Failure to pay on both federal loans and private loans will not only incur substantial fees, but this action will also wreak havoc with your credit score... and it can take a long time to build it back up. In addition, very frequently,*

*your parents co-signed your private loans with
you. Therefore, failure to pay responsibly on
private loans could damage their credit as well.*

Hopefully, you have been paying on these loans while in
school. While private loans may seem like they are "free"
until after you graduate, they are not. Private loans tend
to accrue any unpaid interest rather than pay it for you
(like subsidized federal loans). This accrued interest
works just like the compounding returns example utilized
in the prologue, but in reverse! And unfortunately, the
rates on private loans may be much higher than those
typically seen on federal loans. Regardless, the point is,
if you have private loans, you will want to pay them off
as soon as possible. In my mind, private loans are a better
deal than carrying credit card debt, but not by much.
Dedicate yourself to getting rid of this debt as quickly as
you can.

Consolidating your private debt

In some cases, you can lower your average interest rate on
your private loans by consolidating your loans into one.
Check out the "student loan refinance" link on the SoFi
website (www.sofi.com) for more information. Many
times, loan consolidation companies like SoFi and
CommonBond can provide you with better terms than the
individual loans from other private lenders; particularly if
your credit score is higher now than when you took out
the loans. In addition, if you are financially responsible
about maintaining an adequate checking account balance,
you may want to consider signing up for automatic
payments once your loans are consolidated. In many
instances, a company like SoFi will lower your interest
rate even more if you sign up for this feature.

NOTE: *Sometimes, I've heard of recent graduates consolidating their federal debt as well. This action may provide you with lower monthly payments, but I'm a little skeptical about this being a good idea. If you decide to consolidate your federal loans with a company like SoFi, be sure you understand what you are doing.*

It all goes back to your budget

For most recent graduates with student debt (substantial or otherwise), there is no magic pill that can make it go away. The key to financial success in this area is the same key that's been suggested before. Work hard, get ahead, live within your means, and be smart when it comes to allocating more dollars to one goal verses another. Do these things, and the goal of paying off your debt, as with all your other financial goals will be met with success.

◆ † ◆

♦ CHAPTER TEN ♦

AUTOS & HOUSING

My uncle was definitely a "car guy". Over his lifetime, he owned more cars than he could count. He would buy old, beat-up jalopies, fix them up, and sell them for a tidy profit. If you have a similar skill, then perhaps you will want to revisit chapter two on entrepreneurship. For now though, I tell you this story to state explicitly that this is the exception to the rule when it comes to cars. Automobiles are usually awful investments. If something is a bad investment, being an "investments guy", then I'm typically not a big fan. Therefore, the bulk of my thoughts on the topic of autos are going to be centered on getting you what you need, while at the same time limiting their negative influence on your finances.

Automobile research

When choosing a vehicle, my advice is that your first thought be toward the affordability of it. Do some on-line research on at least a few vehicles that you like to determine which one may be a better value. The Kelley Blue Book site (www.kbb.com) is a fantastic place to get started. Edmunds (www.edmunds.com) is another great source. These sites, as well as others (like www.cargurus.com) can break down the cost of owning the vehicle to impressively specific figures. They also give you an idea of what would be a good deal on the vehicle you want.

Automobile financing

If you can afford the vehicle without taking a loan, then you may just want to pay cash for it. However, if you need a loan to afford the car of your dreams, then next comes the budgeting. You must be sure you can afford the down payment (a lump sum you must put "down" at the initial purchase) and the monthly loan payments. Loan payments will include "principal" which is money that is used to partially pay down what you owe, and "interest" which is profit for the lender. Keep in mind that if you have a poor credit rating and financial history, then the lender is going to want you to pay higher interest. If your credit score is too low, then they may not agree to give you the loan at all.

In fact, it is a good idea to contact your bank (or preferably your credit union) to discuss the size of the loan you need and the associated payments prior to visiting a dealership. If the terms fit within your budget, then go ahead and get pre-qualified for the loan. Your bank or credit union can actually write you a letter that states their intention to lend you the money which may help later with your negotiation.

You typically do not want to use the financing plan offered to you by the vehicle dealer if you can avoid it. Don't be fooled if the dealership acts like they don't understand why you won't take them up on their offer to help you finance your vehicle purchase… They do this because it is quite possible that they make more money from the financing than from the car itself. While there may be the infrequent exception, the terms offered by the automobile dealer's financing company are generally much less friendly (with much higher interest) than if you can qualify for a loan from your credit union. Better yet – like I mentioned before, save up enough so that you don't even need a loan before purchasing the vehicle…

New cars, used cars and leases

Another factor in your decision should be the vehicle's operating costs (fuel, tires, insurance, maintenance, etc.). Because of the potential operating costs, I don't always suggest a used car over a new car, but I definitely lean that way. Typically, (though there have been exceptions) you get more car for your money buying a used or pre-owned car rather than a new car. However, consider the warranties and incentives offered by new car dealers. A new car could make sense, but I kind of doubt it. Regardless, keep your vehicle serviced regularly (oil changes, tire rotations, etc.). This can seem like a lot of out-of-pocket expense if you aren't a "do-it-yourself" person, but it is much less costly than letting your vehicle get to the point that it needs a major overhaul because of your inattention. The financially responsible thing to do is to keep this vehicle for many, many years. Some people may tell you that when it starts needing repairs, it's time to sell it and get another… I'm not one of these people… I think people use that as an excuse to get a new car and I'm not falling for it. Repair it and keep going.

Leasing a car almost never makes financial sense. If you lease a vehicle, you do not own it. You agree to make payments for a certain period of time at which point, the dealer takes the vehicle back. However, leasing is currently really popular because it makes you feel like you have a lower payment – but it's not a payment – it's just an expense. If you can only afford to lease the vehicle you desire (according to your budget) then it's my opinion that you shouldn't get it. Many people really don't like it when I tell them this… Sorry, but my thinking would be that you need to find a less costly vehicle (perhaps an older model) and utilize a loan from your credit union to buy it – not lease it.

Automobile insurance

Most states have compulsory auto insurance (which means coverage is required by law). It is strongly advised that you have automobile insurance on your vehicle. If you don't, you are taking a huge risk every time you drive the vehicle. If you cause an accident, you may end up paying fines, penalties, your expenses and the other party's expenses.

Most states have their own mandatory minimum coverage which differs from state to state. Your property and casualty insurance agent will be able to help you understand the coverage that you need in your state. Speaking of insurance agents – be sure to shop around and obtain quotes from as many insurers as you can find. The premium costs can be substantially different from insurer to insurer. Also be aware that premiums will likely be lower if you have a good driving history, and a lower-priced vehicle.

You may find insurers who describe their policies by giving you three numbers; for instance: 50/100/15. They talk this way with each other often, and I think they forget that the average person doesn't know this terminology... Here is the code for my example (50/100/15): The first number is the limit on payments to one person in an accident ($50,000). The second number is the limit on payments to all persons in an accident ($100,000) and the third number is the limit on payment for damage to others' property ($15,000).

Housing

Unlike most automobiles, a house (or real estate) can be a fantastic investment. You can also lose your shirt. Many homeowners saw the value of their homes crash in the housing crisis of 2008. Many people still owe more on their mortgage (the loan they have on their home) than the house is even worth (sometimes referred to as being underwater). However, post crisis, it is quite possible that a house may still prove to be a great investment.

Renting vs buying

Generally, owning a home is going to be a better financial choice than renting. However, there are some very good reasons to rent.

- If you don't have enough money for a down payment on a home, then renting is a viable option. For most homebuyers, it makes sense to put down at least 20% of the value of the home. Therefore, on a $200,000 home, the down payment would be $40,000... This percentage is considered adequate to preclude you from having to buy extra insurance on the home known as "private mortgage insurance" (PMI) which is a good thing.

- Perhaps you don't like (or can't handle) the responsibilities that come with owning a home. Keeping a yard and house can be a lot of work. No one is going to mow your lawn except you (unless you pay them). There is no "manager" you can call to come fix something when it breaks. It's your responsibility.

- If you are still unsettled then renting is a viable option. You don't want to buy a house if you are moving soon or moving around often. Oftentimes, people your age are not at a very stable point in their lives yet.

- Even though some people have no plans to move, they are just uncomfortable with the perceived permanency of owning a home. This isn't a great financial reason, but if it makes you uncomfortable to buy a home, then don't do it.

NOTE: *If renting makes sense for you, then strongly consider purchasing renter's insurance. The owner of your building is responsible for insuring the building, but not your stuff. Renter's insurance can also protect you from some lawsuits and other claims. Renter's insurance is typically not very expensive.*

Affording a home

The first step to buying a home is figuring out what you can afford. Just like with the automobile, you need to pull out your budget. However, this is going to be just a little trickier than the vehicle. There are a few extra considerations with home purchases.

You may be looking at a real estate website (like www.realtor.com) that does you the service of calculating payments for you. Generally, these payment calculations only include the Principal and Interest on a projected loan (the terms of which you may or may not qualify). However, with a mortgage payment, Taxes and Insurance will also be included in your monthly payment (PITI). You should be able to find an estimate of the real estate taxes for your desired property on-line. Specifically, look up the county or city website for the area where the property resides. For the insurance estimate, contact the insurance agent that you use for your automobile first. He/she is likely going to be able to "bundle" a discount for you that may be a better deal than other insurance agents can offer.

NOTE: *This is just for your estimation. Before pulling the trigger, contact at least a few other agents in your area to obtain homeowners insurance quotes. Don't get lazy. Every dollar counts.*

Other considerations that you should account for in your budget are possible increases in monthly utilities. Also consider allocating estimates for maintenance and repairs. Let me state from personal experience, that these can be significant.

Real estate brokers

In purchasing (and for that matter – selling) a home, there are professionals who can help. You can contact a real estate broker (or agent), who is licensed to represent you when it comes to a home purchase. They can help you by sharing their knowledge, experience, and connections with you. In addition, if you contract with your own real estate broker, they will be able to show you all the homes in the area. Good ones will also be able to point out interesting things about the different properties. This may aid you significantly in your decision process. In addition to helping you find a house that meets your needs, a good real estate broker can actually use their skills to help you negotiate a better deal, thus saving you money. However, they don't do it for free. They won't cost anything up front, but they are paid a percentage from the proceeds of the sale of the home (a commission). There are some inherent conflicts of interest with real estate brokers, but my advice is that if you don't really know what you are doing – get one to help you.

Qualifying for a mortgage

Your bank (as well as many other banks) will have someone during regular business hours who is ready to talk to you about qualifying for a mortgage. However, without a strong credit history, qualifying for a mortgage can be tough. Your credit score is likely going to be the first thing your lender checks. Assuming that looks okay, your lender is still likely to ask you for most of the documents that I asked you to get together in chapter three for your balance sheet and budget. Just like you, they will also need to be sure that you can afford the loan. After the housing fiasco of 2008, this process is now taken very seriously. Once you check out okay, the lender will then conduct on appraisal on the house you want. Just like you, they want to be sure the place is in good shape. If it all looks good – then prepare to sign your name about 50 times. I'm not kidding… there is a lot of paperwork that you will need to sign to get the loan.

Types of mortgages

A conventional mortgage has a fixed interest rate over the

life of the loan and level payments. The principal and interest never change. But note that your payments may change because of changes in your taxes and insurance. If you qualify for a conventional mortgage, it is likely going to be your best bet.

Lenders and homeowners got into trouble in 2008 because they got too fancy. Some adjustable rate mortgages (ARMs) gave people very low "teaser" rates at the start of the loan, and later, when they increased significantly, the homeowner could no longer afford to make the payments – and the housing markets crashed. In addition to adjustable rate mortgages, also be leery if your lender uses the terms balloon mortgage or graduated payment mortgages. These can sometimes seem like good deals to start – but they come back to bite you later.

Length of the mortgage

The typical mortgage is for either 15 or 30 years. You can usually get a lower interest rate on the 15-year loan, but the required payments are somewhat larger than the 30-year loan since you are paying the loan off in half the time. Once again, you will need to check your budget to see which option makes sense for you.

In the past, I have advised financially responsible homebuyers to take the 30-year mortgage even if they can afford the 15-year mortgage. However, even though they have the option of paying lower monthly (30-year) payments, I recommend that they make the payments as if it were a 15-year mortgage. For instance, a 30-year loan may have monthly payments of $1,000 whereas a 15-year loan on the same property would be $1,450. My advice might be to take the 30-year loan, but still pay $1,450 each month. This strategy can provide responsible homeowners with a way to pay off their home relatively quickly, but still provide them with the flexibility to lower their monthly mortgage payments if an emergency or other need/opportunity arises. In this example, the homebuyer could technically cut his/her monthly expenses by $450 if there was a need. Had the buyer taken the 15-year mortgage, the lender would likely "insist" on the $1,450 payment...

NOTE: *If you are considering this option, be sure to check with your lender to see if there is any "prepayment" penalty. In most cases, you can pay off the loan as quickly as you like, but some lenders may try to sneak a stipulation into your loan terms that prevents it. If they do – my strong advice would be to try to find another lender.*

◆ † ◆

♦ CHAPTER ELEVEN ♦

INVESTING BASICS

There is an episode of "South Park" where Stan meets his future "self" though time travel and determines that the "future Stan" is a loser. It turns out to be a scam perpetrated by Stan's parents to get him to not do drugs, but the thought of meeting my "future-self" stuck with me after seeing the episode. The next day, I was advising a student, named Matt, on his senior year. I told him that he had two options. The first option would be to spread his courses out evenly over his remaining two semesters, or, he could do "future-Matt" a favor and load up in the fall semester, making for an easy spring. He smiled and told me he wanted to do "future-Matt" a favor. He loaded up and enjoyed a carefree spring send-off semester from college.

Matt was doing his future-self a favor, but he was only looking a semester ahead. I think it might be easier to do your future-self a favor when the timeframe is short. I might wash the dishes before I go to bed, so I don't have to get up in the morning and do them. I know what I'm like in the morning. I know I'll be glad I did them. You probably know your short-term future-self as well as I know mine.

However, do we know what we'll be like 30 or 40 years from now? I really have no idea. It's harder to do someone a favor when you don't know them – isn't it... So, many of us don't. We might mow the lawn Thursday to free up our weekend, but we don't do any favors for our long-term future-selves.

Do you know who can maybe get away with this short-term thinking? People who have other people to take care of them. No one is going to take care of you – Except you! But here is the catch – in order to do it, the today-you must take care of the future-you.

Take a moment and imagine that a time machine has been invented, and in a few hours, you are going to get a visit from your 65-year old self. Will they like you? – your choices? What advice do you think they will have for you? Is one of those bits of advice to invest for your future? I think you know the answer...

Thus far, the advice and recommendations in this book have been designed to get your "today-self" in financial order. You can't build a house unless you've laid the foundation. Now that the foundation has been established (with a healthy budget, paid-off credit cards, etc.) let's look forward and do your future-self a favor.

Overview of investments

When it comes to investing, you can invest in both real assets and financial assets. A real asset would be something like a McDonald's restaurant while a financial asset would be McDonald's stock. With a financial asset, you don't have any day-to-day responsibilities. You let other people run the business; you just own some of it. In this chapter, we are going to limit our discussion to financial assets (we discussed some real assets back in chapter two and three).

We are also going to primarily limit our discussion of asset categories to the following:

Common stocks:

Represent ownership in a corporation. Like I mentioned above, you can buy stock in McDonalds that entitles you to your share of McDonalds' profits. There are literally thousands of companies in which you can buy stock. You probably know many of the "big" companies, but may not know some of the smaller companies. In fact, to aid our discussion, let's further divide stocks into the following categories:

Company size:

- *Large-cap stock* – U.S. companies with market capitalizations over $10 billion (Example: Apple, Comcast, Proctor & Gamble)

- *Mid-cap stock* – U.S. companies with market capitalizations between $2 billion & $10 billion (Example: American Eagle, Domino's Pizza, Universal Health Services)

- *Small-cap stock* – U.S. companies with market capitalizations under $2 billion (Example: BJ's Restaurants, iRobot, HMS Holding)

Geographic location:

- *International stock* – Non-U.S. companies from "advanced" countries (Example: Japan, Europe)

- *Emerging markets stock* – Non-U.S. companies from countries that are progressing toward becoming an advanced economy (Example: Taiwan, Brazil)

Bonds:

Represent a loan you have made to another entity (government, municipality, or a corporation). Bonds are "debt". As the lender, you are typically entitled to receive interest on the loan and you hope to get your loaned money back at the end of the loan period. To aid our discussion, let's further divide bonds into the following categories:

Maturity date (length of the loan period):

- *Short-term bond* - Matures within two years

- *Intermediate-term bond* - Matures between two and ten years

- *Long-term bond* - Matures in more than ten years

Type of entity issuing the debt:

- *Government bond* – Debt that is backed by the U.S. Government (Treasuries)

- o All U.S. issued debt is considered high-quality

- *Corporate bond* – Debt that is issued by a company and sold to the public
  - o Corporate debt could be high, mid, or low-quality depending on the reputation of the company

Cash and money markets:

In "investments", cash is typically a money market fund (discussed in chapter five). I know that the money you carry in your pocket is also called cash – but that is not what we are talking about in this chapter. "Cash" is a debt that is to be paid back in a manner of days. Since the debt is so short-term, it is considered very safe. It will collect some interest, but not very much.

Ways to make money by investing

For our purposes, investing is all about the future, but investments can provide both current and future income. There are two basic ways that investments are going to make you money.

- Money you earn while you own the investment (interest, dividends)

- Money you earn from selling the investment for more than you paid for it (capital gain)

In your investments, you can take any current money you make and re-invest it. This provides you with the power of compounding that we discussed way back in the prologue.

Investment returns

Speaking of the prologue, do you remember Bob and Sue? Remember Sue invested today and Bob waited 10 years and Sue came out way ahead? If you look at that example again, you will notice that each of them earned 9% per year on their investments. To be completely honest, there is no investment I know of that earns that high of a rate of return consistently every year. However, it may be possible to invest in financial assets that earn an "average return" of 9% per year over a number of years. Average returns may never be 9% in any given year, but average out to be 9% over time.

As an example, Exhibit 11-A lists the annual returns and the growth of a $1,000 investment for the S&P 500 index from 2003 through 2017 (15 years).

NOTE: The S&P 500 is a combination of (pretty much) the 500 largest companies in America. Investing in the S&P 500 means that you own stock in these 500 companies. The S&P 500 is a very popular "investment benchmark" that many investors use to measure their personal performance while investing in large-cap stocks. If you want to invest in the S&P 500, it is actually very simple, and will be discussed later.

Doing the math, if you had invested $1,000 at the beginning of 2003, your money would have grown to just over $4,000 by the end of 2017. Thus, the geometric average return per year was approximately 9.8%. *Assuming no fees of course, but more on that later...*

EXHIBIT 11-A – Annual Returns and Growth of $1,000 in the S&P 500

Year	S&P 500 Return	Investment of $1,000
2003	28.68%	$1,286.80
2004	10.88%	$1,426.80
2005	04.91%	$1,496.86
2006	15.79%	$1,733.21
2007	05.49%	$1,828.37
2008	-37.00%	$1,151.87
2009	26.46%	$1,456.66
2010	15.06%	$1,676,03
2011	02.11%	$1,711.39
2012	16.00%	$1,985.22
2013	32.39%	$2,628.23
2014	13.69%	$2,988.03
2015	01.38%	$3,029.27
2016	11.96%	$3,391.57
2017	21.83%	$4,131.95

Return figures obtained from www.vanguard.com

Looking at our table of historical S&P 500 returns, none of the individual years had a return of 9.8%, but had we invested at the beginning of 2003, our average compound return from 2003 to 2017 would have been 9.8%.

That "return" is very important to you as an investor. The higher your return, the more your money grows. The higher the return, the more your money is working for you (and possibly – the less you have to work). Other things equal – the higher your return – the better. Unfortunately, other things are not equal.

The risk/return tradeoff

Typically, the higher the return we strive to obtain in our investing, the greater the risk to our investments. While there are many types of investment risk, we are going to only focus on volatility. For just a moment, go back and look at the returns of the S&P 500 for 2007 – 2009. This was a volatile period! With the financial crisis that we had in 2008, if you were invested in the S&P 500 – you lost a lot of money! No one really cares about volatility when it is associated with an upswing (like we had in 2009). However, everybody cares about the volatile down-swings. These can be tough to take!

Think about volatility like surfing waves at the beach:

A low risk/low return investment strategy is an option that is like surfing a calm sea. You can catch a wave without much excitement. You can ride your little wave all the way into the shore, but it might take you a while as you aren't going very fast. You can still wipe out, but it's not going to hurt too badly. If you fall, you likely won't get knocked over by another wave. You can stand up pretty easily and catch the next one.

- Here are some investments that match this strategy. We will typically get more and more risky with higher return potential as we go down the list:

    o Cash (include Money markets, Short-term U.S. Government Bonds or T-bills)
    o Intermediate-term U.S. Government Bonds
    o Long-term U.S. Government Bonds
    o High-quality Corporate Bonds

A high risk/high return investment strategy is the sea after a storm. The waves are big! Catching one can be a little scary, but when you are up and riding the wave, it is exhilarating. You finish more quickly, because you are travelling fast. However, if you wipe out – it hurts! You are going to get knocked around. Even worse, once you get your bearings, sometimes you are liable to get knocked over again by another wave. Unfortunately though, there is no way to catch an impressive wave without accepting the risks associated with it.

- Here are some investments that match this strategy. We will typically get more and more risky with higher return potential as we go down the list:

    o Large-cap Stocks
    o Mid-cap Stocks
    o Small-cap Stocks
    o International Stocks
    o Emerging market Stocks

What kind of wave rider are you? If you like the calm seas, you may want to invest in short-term bonds. If you want to catch a gnarly one, then you might want to invest in small-cap stocks. Let's look in a little greater detail at just these two options. In fact, let's look at them over the exact same time period that we looked at the S&P 500. In order to represent the returns of short-term bonds, we will use a short-term bond index (Barclays) and a small-cap growth index (Russell 2500) will represent the returns of small cap stocks.

As you can see in Exhibit 11-B, a $1,000 investment in 2003 in the short-term bond index would have grown to $1,522 by the end of 2017. The same $1,000 in the small-cap growth index would have grown to $5,594!

EXHIBIT 11-B – Annual Returns and Growth of $1,000 in the Barclay's Short-term Bond Index & the Russell 2500 (Small-cap) Growth Index

Year	Barclays S-T Bond Index	Growth of $1,000	Russell 2500 Growth Index	Growth of $1,000
2003	3.35%	$1,034	46.31%	$1,463
2004	1.85%	$1,053	14.59%	$1,677
2005	1.44%	$1,068	08.17%	$1,814
2006	4.22%	$1,113	12.26%	$2,036
2007	7.27%	$1,194	09.69%	$2,233
2008	5.12%	$1,255	-41.50%	$1,306
2009	4.62%	$1,313	41.66%	$1,851
2010	4.08%	$1,366	28.86%	$2,385
2011	3.13%	$1,409	-01.57%	$2,347
2012	2.24%	$1,441	16.13%	$2,726
2013	0.29%	$1,445	40.65%	$3,834
2014	1.43%	$1,466	07.05%	$4,104
2015	0.97%	$1,480	-00.19%	$4,097
2016	1.57%	$1,503	09.79%	$4,495
2017	1.29%	$1,522	24.46%	$5,594

Return figures obtained from www.vanguard.com

Looking at only this one example, it may seem like the riskier small-cap growth investment is a no-brainer. More money is better – right? Let me caution you that the absolute worst thing you can do is think you are a big wave rider – when you really aren't. You have to know you can handle the wave! If you can't, you are going to get hurt. Let me explain what I mean.

I have known many people who see tables like this and start their investment strategy by investing aggressively.

They think they can handle the down years. Then, we get a year like 2008 and they lose 40% of their money. Whoa!!! Turns out they were not an aggressive investor after all. So, what they do then is take their money out of the small-cap growth investment and put it in the short-term bond investment. This is basically the worst thing they can do. They are "locking in" the loss. But in the fear of the moment, they just can't help themselves.

Recently, I was engaged in some small talk with a nurse at my doctor's office. When she found out what I did for a living, she began to tell me about the "horrible" investment advisor she had. "He had us in investments that lost half their value in the financial crisis, so we found ourselves another advisor." I asked if they had made their money back yet. "No – of course not! Our new advisor has us in much safer investments."

If the nurse (who was a super nice lady – BTW) had stuck it out with the old advisor's investment strategy, she would have made her money back and made a lot more money on top of that. But, she wasn't a big wave rider. She locked in her loss, and now, many years later, she is still worse off because of it. It would have been better to have either caught a small wave from the beginning – or ridden out the big wave – but people's minds just don't work like that. In investing, most people's instinct is completely wrong. Don't let this be you.

Isn't there a middle ground?

Okay – so maybe you aren't a big wave rider, but you don't think you want to wade around in the kiddie pool either. Is there a middle ground? Absolutely!

When you mix different asset classes (large-cap, mid-cap, small-cap, government bonds, corporate bonds, etc.) you are engaging in what we call a diversification strategy – and it is a good thing. In the investment industry, advisors and academics have a hard time agreeing on anything as "certain". However, practically the entire investment community agrees that diversification is smart. Therefore, you should strongly consider diversifying your own investments.

- If you think you lean toward the more conservative side, then you will weight your portfolio with lower risk/lower return investments.

- If you think you are a more aggressive investor, then you will weight your portfolio toward the higher risk/higher return investments.

NOTE: *Most young investors (like yourself) tend to invest more aggressively than older investors. You have more time to recover if you have a bad year or two. But it's entirely up to you. Just because you can, doesn't mean you should!*

Okay – makes sense – but how do I do it?

You've been given a lot of information to digest in this chapter. You may feel like you kind of know about the different asset classes and your wave riding nature. But you may be completely clueless on how exactly you would go about investing in a well-diversified portfolio of stocks and bonds. If this is the case – you are right where you should be. Keep reading…

There are two really easy and efficient ways to invest in the market; mutual funds and exchange-traded funds. Let's focus first on mutual funds.

Imagine that you (and several thousand friends of yours) send money to a guy named Bill to hold for you. This guy, Bill, knows a lot about investing, so he takes your (and all your thousands of friend's) money and invests it in stocks and bonds. Then, every year, Bill reports to you how much he has been able to make (or how much he's lost). By the way, since Bill is doing all this for you, he keeps just a little bit of your money each year for his trouble. This arrangement with Bill is kind of how a mutual fund works. The decision then becomes – who are you going to pick for your "Bill"?

Mutual funds

There are thousands of mutual funds and many you can invest in on-line (once you've got your bank account – see chapter four). Here is an extremely partial list of mutual fund families. They all have websites so you can check them out if you'd like more information on any of them.

Within each fund family, there may be many different funds that have different investment goals. Some funds invest in only mid-cap stocks, or corporate bonds, etc. You can find a fund that limits its investments to any of the asset classes that we've previously discussed. Other funds might combine asset classes to make for a more "diversified" fund. Other funds, known as balanced funds actually invest in stocks and bonds at the same time. There are thousands of options!

Sixteen Popular Mutual Fund Families

AIM	American Century
Black Rock	Dreyfus
Eaton Vance	Fidelity
Franklin Templeton	Goldman Sachs
Invesco	Janus
MFS	PIMCO
Putnam	Royce
State Street	Vanguard

I have personally chosen Vanguard mutual funds for most of my mutual fund investment dollars. I like them because in my personal research, Vanguard has the lowest expenses of any mutual fund family (more about expenses shortly). Let me state that I have no affiliation with Vanguard except for the fact that I own several of their mutual funds. However, given my personal affinity and knowledge of Vanguard, I'm going to limit my examples to Vanguard mutual funds.

NOTE: *You may like another fund family better than Vanguard. I think that is great! I just want you to invest!!!*

My friend, Jan, is 26 years old and has a fairly aggressive risk tolerance (she can handle volatility and is in it for the long haul). She put together the following allocation:

NOTE: *The percentages in Jan's portfolio represent the percentage of her total investment dollars she has allocated to each fund. For example, if Jan had $10,000 total – she's got $4,000 in the S&P 500 fund, $1,500 in the Mid-Cap Index fund, etc.*

Jan's Moderately Aggressive Allocation

Fund	Percentage Allocation
Vanguard S&P 500 *(large cap)*	40%
Vanguard Mid-Cap Index	15%
Vanguard Small-Cap Index	15%
Vanguard Total International Stock Index	15%
Vanguard Emerging Markets Stock Index	5%
Vanguard Inter-Term Corporate Bond	10%

Another friend, Jessica, is 31 years old and has a much less aggressive risk tolerance than Jan. She wants a decent return over the long term, but she doesn't want to endure the volatility of Jan's aggressive portfolio. She has the following allocation:

Jessica's More Conservative Allocation

Fund	Percentage Allocation
Vanguard S&P 500 *(large cap)*	30%
Vanguard Explorer *(mid/small stock)*	15%
Vanguard Total International Stock Index	10%
Vanguard Inter-Term Corporate Bond	20%
Vanguard Inter-Term Govt. Bond	20%
Vanguard Short-Term Federal Bond	5%

NOTE: Let me be absolutely clear – neither of these portfolios is a recommendation! These are just two portfolios that happen to match the risk tolerance, investment goals, time horizons, and financial needs of two randomly chosen people. You need to do your own research and create your own portfolio (or hire a financial advisor to help you – see chapter thirteen).

You may notice that many of the above funds are called "index" funds. An index fund is a passively-managed fund. The manager of the fund doesn't try to pick and choose stocks and bonds to put in the fund. They just invest in an already existing index. These funds tend to have lower fees than actively-managed funds (see below). For more information on this topic, I suggest you check out "A Random Walk Down Wall Street" by Burton Malkiel. It's a fantastic read.

The "buy it & forget it" option

Several mutual fund families (including Vanguard) have what they call "Target Date" or "Target Retirement" funds. These funds are what I would call "buy it and forget it" funds. Once you purchase the fund, you really don't have to think about it again – ever.

For instance, I assume you have roughly 40 years or so before retirement in the year 2060. Vanguard has a fund called "Target Retirement 2060" which offers you a diversified portfolio that will adjust its underlying assets over time. Today, the fund is heavily invested in different types of stocks (with less in bonds). However, as you get older, the fund will gradually move your money out of stocks, and into bonds. This typically fits many investors' investment objective of becoming more conservative, the closer they get to retirement... Like I said – buy it and forget it. Unlike Jan and Jessica, you wouldn't really have to worry about putting your own portfolio together. You could just let the mutual fund company do it for you.

Mutual fund expenses

One of my largest criteria when selecting a mutual fund is being sure I'm not paying too much for it. Mutual funds have several different types of expenses, but there are only a few things for which you need to be on the lookout:

1. **Look for funds that are classified as "no load".**

   - "Load" funds have up-front or back-end fees. They are becoming less popular, but there are still many out there. I'd recommend you avoid paying a load.

2. **Try to avoid funds with "12b-1" fees.**

   - You probably don't know or care what this is – but 12b-1 fees are marketing and distribution fees that the fund is allowed to charge. The mutual fund prospectus will blatantly state weather or not the fund has these fees (regulations force mutual fund companies to make it obvious). There are plenty of funds that don't have this fee. I'd recommend you avoid paying a 12b-1 fee.

3. **Keep an eye on the "management" fees.**

   - Compare the management fees of the funds you like within the same asset category (i.e. – Small-cap). Consider choosing the less expensive one for your portfolio. Management fees (like 12b-1 fees) are going to be obviously stated in the literature available on the fund. This is why I like Vanguard. Of all the mutual funds I've looked at, Vanguard consistently has the lowest fees.

4. **If given the option between "TF" and "NTF" – go with "NTF".**

    - If you buy mutual funds directly from the mutual fund family's website, you won't have to worry about "TF – Transaction Fee" and "NTF – No Transaction Fee". However, if you set up a brokerage account at a "financial supermarket" like Charles Schwab or Scottrade, then you will want to keep an eye out for these extra fees.

Setting up your account

For help on the actual process of setting up a brokerage account, see the section in chapter thirteen on setting up an on-line account. Once the set-up process is complete, to get started investing in mutual funds, you are going to be asked how you plan to fund the account. You typically have the option to mail them a check or to set up your account to transfer funds electronically from your bank. Electronic transfers can be a little tricky to set up (because of the extreme care the brokerage takes to protect your account against fraud), but may be worth it over the long run. While you have the option of investing directly in a mutual fund, I'd suggest that you consider depositing funds in a money market mutual fund (discussed in chapter four) first.

From the money market fund, you can then quickly and easily move money into your stock and bond mutual fund selections. The reason I suggest using the money market fund is because if you have the bank wire the money into the fund directly, you may find that it is sent on a day when the market is way up. I personally wouldn't really like this... I'd wait for a day when markets are down and dragging. Better yet, I might wait for them to be down for a few days… In the realm of it all, this strategy has almost zero impact on my long-term returns. However, psychologically, I feel so much better if I feel like I can time my purchase for a day when the market is "on sale". Sometimes in investing, I'm not sure it is a bad thing to play some mind games with yourself like this.

NOTE: *You can see how the market is doing anytime on television (CNBC, Fox Business, etc.) or on the Internet (Yahoo Finance, MSN Money, etc.)*

       Don't get too fixated on the timing. You can wait yourself out of some awesome growth if you are not careful. Also – there is no need to try to time your mutual fund purchase to the minute. All mutual fund transactions are closed out as of the market close on the day you buy them.

Investment minimums

One down side to mutual fund investing is the fact that mutual funds have a minimum amount that they require before they will allow you to invest. For instance, most Vanguard funds require at least $3,000 of an initial minimum investment. However, once you meet the initial minimum requirement, most funds then allow you to save additional amounts as low as $50 or $100. In fact, some other fund families may have initial minimum initial investments as low as $100 – if you establish an automatic investment plan – which may not be a bad idea.

NOTE: *These minimums will not be an issue if you are saving into your company's retirement plan (discussed in the next chapter). Your company*

*sponsored retirement plan funds will have no
initial minimum.*

Getting around investment minimums with ETFs

Exchange-traded funds (or ETFs for short) are very
similar to index mutual funds. However, ETFs share
some qualities with stocks when it comes to the way they
trade. The first ETF ever created back in 1993 was an
S&P 500 Index fund (nicknamed "Spider" because of the
SPDR ticker symbol). ETFs have grown considerably in
their popularity since then, and today, you can find an
ETF that tracks just about any index or sector associated
with the market.

Since the ETF is traded like a stock, the trading expenses
are very similar to that of a stock (rather than a mutual
fund). With most ETFs, buyers and sellers pay a
commission for the trade which can vary substantially
depending on the broker. ETFs have no loads or 12b-1
fees and the management expenses for ETFs are typically
much lower than that of mutual funds. In fact, the
management fees for ETFs are typically even lower than
that of low-cost index mutual funds.

If you have a strong desire to invest, but currently have an
extremely limited budget, ETFs typically have no
investment minimum. You can buy as little as one share
of most ETFs. But keep in mind that (in most cases) you
will be paying a commission which can have a profound
impact on small investment dollar amounts. For instance,
if you pay a $10 commission on a purchase of $1,000 –
your commission is only 1% of your purchase. However,
if you pay a $10 commission on a $100 purchase, you are
paying 10% of your purchase! With this sort of impact, it
might make sense to save up more money before investing

in an ETF. Also keep in mind that you will need to pay that commission again when you sell the ETF.

NOTE: *If you open up a brokerage account at Vanguard, you can trade Vanguard ETFs with no commissions. I understand the same is true if you open up a Fidelity account and only trade Fidelity ETFs. Other brokerages may provide the same commission-free trading.*

There is a relatively new brokerage option that has been growing in popularity, primarily with younger investors, because of its low fees and ease of use. Robinhood (www.robinhood.com) is a brokerage app that lets you buy and sell U.S. listed stocks and ETFs with $0 commission. Unfortunately, you cannot purchase mutual funds on Robinhood at this time, and the app may have limited flexibility when compared to a more traditional brokerage. However, for those interested in getting started in investing with a small amount of money – this may be your best bet.

Dollar cost averaging

Once you have your mutual fund and/or ETF portfolio, it is generally wise to force yourself to save regularly into them. This strategy involves buying a fixed dollar amount of the mutual fund/ETF on a regular schedule, regardless of the share price. For instance, if you regularly save $10 from your paycheck into your company's 401(k) then you are dollar cost averaging.

Psychologically, this can be a load off. Assume for a moment that you are dollar cost averaging $10 every

Friday into a stock mutual fund. Let's further assume that your investments have been going down, and you are generally bummed about that. But perking you up is the fact that you know that your next $10 is going to buy investments that are "on sale". You are going to get more for my money. This feels pretty good!

Are mutual funds and ETFs all that you recommend?

It is my personal opinion that new investors should invest at least the first $25,000 of their investment dollars into a diversified portfolio of mutual funds or exchange-traded funds. My personal philosophy to investing is that you buy your "workhorse" before you get a "racehorse". A diversified portfolio of mutual funds/ETFs is my recommendation for your workhorse. In fact, I believe that for many investors, mutual funds and/or ETFs would be all they would ever need to reach their financial goals.

However, racehorses can be fun. Due to the inherent lack of diversification when compared to mutual funds, individual stock investing is more risky than mutual fund investing – but the payoffs can also be greater. If you have your $25,000 workhorse plugging away for you and you want to buy a racehorse, let me recommend that you check out Jim Cramer's book, "Get Rich Carefully". He also has a daily television show and several other books on the topic of "racehorse" investing. He's smart... and fun.

◆ † ◆

♦ CHAPTER TWELVE ♦

USING RETIREMENT PLANS

If you are investing for the long haul, then you need to be utilizing retirement plans. Let's think back for a moment to the earlier chapter on taxes. Specifically, do you remember the income and capital gains taxes? In a regular brokerage account, these two taxes are going to negatively impact your investments.

For instance, let's look at the short-term bond example from the previous chapter. We invested $1,000 in the short-term bond index and 15 years later, the fund had grown to $1,522. Now, let's make it a "real world" example. In the real world – we pay taxes. If we assume that we pay 20% of our income in taxes (not an unreasonable assumption) then instead of growing to $1,522 – our account only grows to $1,401.

In summary, over the 15 years, we earn $522 in interest, but we pay $121 in taxes over that time, so we only end up making $401.

This is kind of uncool, isn't it? You are being responsible and doing what you are supposed to be doing (saving for your future) and the government appears to be punishing you for that!

Before I get you too riled up, let me explain that it is my belief that our government does want you to save for your future and be successful. They have set up some perfectly legal ways for you to avoid paying these particular taxes. You just have to follow a few rules.

A tax umbrella

I saw a girl the other day wearing a shirt that proclaimed "I'm so sweet, I melt in the rain". I doubted this was true. Regardless, the shirt evoked some imagery in my mind of a girl made of sugar and standing in the rain. As the rain comes down, the sugar girl melts away to nothing.

In this metaphor, the girl made of sugar is your investment portfolio and the rain drops are taxes. Taxes will melt away an unprotected investment portfolio. So what do you do to protect your sugar girl (investment portfolio)? You put an umbrella over it. Qualified retirement plans act as an umbrella to protect your portfolio from tax. Let's talk about a few popular options:

What's the rate of return?

Before I get started, let me bring up an often misunderstood aspect of retirement plans. I often get the question – "What is the rate of return on a Roth IRA?" My answer is that it could be anything. A Roth IRA isn't an "investment" like a mutual fund. The Roth IRA is a tax umbrella that you hold over your investment to protect it from being taxed. Your investment could be earning a rate of return of anything. In this chapter, we are not talking about investments (that was chapter eleven). In this chapter, we are talking about tax umbrellas that you can put your investments under.

The 401(k)

If you work for a "for-profit" business, then your employer may provide you the option of saving a portion of your income into the company's 401(k) plan. If you work for a "non-profit" (like me) then instead of calling it a 401(k), it is called a 403(b). Government employees may have the same type of plan, but they call it a 457. These are basically all the same thing – a retirement plan offered to you by your employer with very similar rules. They are all classified under the term "defined contribution" plans because you "define" the amount you are going to "contribute" to your own plan.

NOTE: *The numbers and letters that describe these plans are the sections of the U. S. tax code that describe them.*

If you work for a small company, you may have access to a Simplified Employee Pension (SEP) or a Savings Incentive Match Plan for Employees (SIMPLE). From an employee's perspective, these plans are very similar to a 401(k). They were discussed from the employer's perspective back in chapter two.

The 401(k) is a salary reduction plan which means that any money you save into it comes directly out of your paycheck (pre-tax) and lowers your taxable income. This lowers your tax liability today! In addition, once the money is in under the 401(k) umbrella, it grows tax-deferred until you take it out in retirement. If you remember back to the example I gave at the beginning of this chapter, if your 401(k) had been invested in the short-term bond index, you would not owe tax on any interest – and you would have earned $522 over the 15 years instead of $401.

The primary downside to 401(k) investing is the fact that if you need to take the money out of it before you reach age 59 ½, you incur a penalty tax (in addition to regular income taxes). There is an option to take a loan from your 401(k) that may avoid the penalties, but I'm going to recommend that you not consider this as an option (except for extreme emergencies). Your 401(k) is a long-term retirement vehicle. If you are withdrawing from it, or taking loans against it, then you are not using it for the purpose for which it was designed. Promise yourself that you won't touch this money again until you retire! In fact, the government will actually make you take distributions from your 401(k) after age 70 ½ (these are called required minimum distributions).

401(k) matching contributions

If your company offers you the opportunity of saving into a 401(k), you should probably take it just for the tax benefits. However, let me describe a possible option that makes saving into your 401(k) a "no-brainer". In some 401(k) plans, your employer will actually "match" your contributions. If this is the case, then it's the best deal you've got when it comes to investing. In fact, you may recall from the chapter on credit cards, that this is pretty much the only investment option that makes sense if you carry high-interest credit card debt.

If offered, it is often listed in your benefits handbook as "employer matching". This means that if you save your own money into your 401(k), then your employer will also save their money into your 401(k). The amount depends on the level of the match. For example, your benefits handbook might state the following:

- Example 1: 100% of the first 3% of contributions

What this means is that if you save 3% of your salary into your 401(k), your employer will match you dollar for dollar. Assume your salary is $30,000. If you save $900 per year (3% of your salary) into your 401(k), your employer will also save $900 (100% of 3%).

- Example 2: 50% of the first 6% of contributions

What this means is that if you save 6% of your salary into your 401(k), your employer will match you 50 cents on the dollar. Assume your salary is $30,000. If you save $1,800 per year (6% of your salary) into your 401(k), your employer will save $900 (50% of 6%).

NOTE: *You don't have to save the full percentage of salary if that is not an option for you. If you do this, you are leaving some money on the table, but you are still getting the match on whatever amount you can save. In the previous example (50% on the first 6% of contributions) if your salary was $30,000 and you only saved $1,500 (5% of your salary) into your 401(k), your employer would still save $750 (50% of 5%).*

If you save more than the stated amount – that is awesome! You are generally allowed to save up to $18,500 (in 2018). However, your *employer is only going to match what they state they will match. In the previous example (50% on the first 6% of contributions,) if your salary was $30,000 and you saved $6,000 (20% of your salary) into your 401(k), your employer would only save $900 (50% of 6%).*

My advice is to never leave money on the table. Be sure to always save at least the percentage of your salary that your employer is going to match. What else can you invest in that (in essence) offers you a 100% or 50% return on your money on day one? -- Nothing I know of...

401(k) vesting

It is not odd for companies to require you to work for a certain amount of time before you are eligible to participate in the 401(k) plan (for instance, you may need to work for a company for a year before you are allowed to participate). In addition, occasionally, your employer may require vesting in your matched contributions before you are entitled to them. To be clear, any money you save into your 401(k) is your money; however, if there is a vesting schedule, you may not be entitled to take ownership of your matched contributions until the vesting schedule has been met.

Companies that have a lot of turnover may be more liable to institute a vesting schedule. If your company thinks you might quit after six months, they want a way to get their matching contributions back from you. A vesting schedule allows them to do this.

NOTE: *I've known people who really want to quit their jobs, but they stay for another 6-8 months so they are fully vested in their retirement plans...*

401(k) investment options

In many cases, your employer will offer you a selection of maybe 15 to 30 different mutual fund options from which to choose within your 401(k). Go back and read the chapter on investing for some tips on how to go about choosing a portfolio that might fit your investment goals and risk tolerance. Note that in a 401(k), you do not typically have to worry about investment minimums.

The Individual Retirement Account (IRA)

A Traditional IRA is a personal retirement savings plan. Since it is a "personal" plan, it won't be offered by your employer. You can set this tax umbrella up yourself. However, I'm not going to discuss a Traditional IRA very much, because for almost all young people, I deem the Roth IRA to be a more suitable retirement planning vehicle.

The Roth IRA was established in 1997 by a Senator named William Roth (of Delaware). I feel like we owe this guy, because the Roth IRA is one of the best deals going. A Roth IRA works a little differently from the 401(k). First off, since this is an individual plan, you are not going to have your employer matching any of your contributions. But, you also aren't going to have your employer setting up vesting schedules or limiting who is eligible to participate. Lastly, while most 401(k) plans might have 15 to 30 different mutual funds; in a Roth IRA, you can invest in just about any financial instrument you want.

Why a Roth IRA?

The reason why I think the Roth IRA is so awesome is

because of the tax rules associated with this particular umbrella.

1. When you save into a Roth IRA, you DO NOT get to deduct your savings amount from this year's taxes.

   If you have been paying attention, you know this is not a good thing... Deductions are good. You want deductions – and this umbrella doesn't provide them. Why then do I like the Roth IRA so much??? Keep reading.

2. Any growth on your money, once it is under the Roth IRA umbrella, is not taxed.

   Again, if you've been paying attention, you know that this is the same deal as the 401(k). So what is so special about a Roth IRA???

3. If you do not withdraw the funds from your Roth IRA until after age 59 ½, then you won't owe any taxes on any of it.

   This is the big deal. In every other retirement plan (including a 401(k) or Traditional IRA) you owe taxes on your investment when you make withdrawals in retirement. With a Roth IRA – you do not. If you follow the rules, then you won't have to pay taxes on that money ever.

Let me explain why I think this is such a great idea for young people like you. First off, do you think you are going to make more money this year or in 30 years? Most of you probably feel that you will make more and more money as you progress in your careers and I agree with you. Because of this, I contend that you are likely in a lower tax bracket today than you will be later. Why not go ahead and pay the tax on your money today (in a Roth IRA) so that when you are older (and arguably in a higher tax bracket) you won't have to pay it.

NOTE: *You must have "earned income" to save into a Roth IRA. Basically, what this means is that you have to have a job and earn money. However, if you make too much money, the government will not allow you to fully enjoy all that a Roth IRA has to offer. If you (as a single person) make over $120,000 – then you will need to do some more research to see if you qualify.*

Pensions

You may already be familiar with the term "pension plan". This is a type of retirement plan that your employer funds for you while you work for the firm. At retirement you are then able to draw income from the pension fund. These "defined benefit" plans are great if you can get one, but most of us don't have the option. Public service jobs (working for the local, state, or federal government) are just about the only jobs I know of that still consistently pay pensions.

While these plans are a fantastic benefit to the employee, they proved to be too unprofitable for the company. I'm once again oversimplifying things, but these plans are one of the primary reason that General Motors (GM) went bankrupt several years ago. I heard one television commentator state once that "GM is like a retirement home that also makes some cars on the side".

NOTE: *Do you notice any similarities between pension plans and Social Security benefits?*

Due to the lack of financial feasibility, most firms have completely done away with pensions. In doing so, they have shifted the responsibility of saving for retirement from them to you. In the past, people didn't have to save as much because the company would help take care of them. No one is going to take care of you.

My opinion on successful retirement investing

My best advice to give on successful retirement investing is to save! The more you feel you are able to save into a retirement plan – the better. I have the following priorities when it comes to my retirement investing. You may not have sufficient funds to reach all four priorities. In addition, you may not have access to all these retirement vehicles. For instance, your employer may not offer a retirement plan. This is okay. Meet the ones you can.

Priority One: Save into the employer-sponsored retirement plan (401(k), 403(b), 457) to take full advantage of any employer match.

- I refuse to leave money on the table. If my employer matches anything – I'm going to take full advantage of it.

Priority Two: Save the full amount allowed into a Roth IRA.

- Just like the government limits the amount we are allowed to save into a 401(k) – they also limit the amount we are allowed to save into a Roth IRA. The limit can change every year, but in 2018, it is $5,500. Whatever the limit is… this is my second priority. I want that tax-free money in retirement.

Priority Three: Go back to the employer-sponsored plan and save up to the fully allowed amount.

- If I've met priority one and two, and I still have funds that I wish to allocate to my retirement goal, then I will go back and increase the percentage that I save into my 401(k). I'm not getting a match on these dollars, but I'm still getting the power of tax-deferral.

Priority Four: Assuming there is no permanent need for life insurance, save any additional funds into a taxable account.

- I doubt you will have a need for permanent life insurance, but if you do, see chapter seven, as well as your financial advisor/insurance agent. I do not currently have a need for permanent life insurance, so for the rest of my retirement savings dollars, I save into a regular taxable account of mutual funds/exchange-traded funds and possibly individual stocks and bonds. Since there is no "cap" on the amount I can save into my taxable account – this becomes the final priority.

How much do you need to save?

I wish I had a good rule of thumb for you here, but I don't. Your needs in retirement are totally dependent on what you want to do in retirement. You might be perfectly fine if you are able to save $1,000,000 by age 65 (which may safely provide approximately $50,000 of income per year). On the other hand, you might run out of money even if you saved $10,000,000 by age 65. There is no good rule of thumb. My advice is to meet with your financial advisor to determine an amount specific to your needs. In my humble opinion though, if you are able to meet my first two retirement priorities (matched 401(k) and a fully-funded Roth IRA), then I think you are doing pretty well (though I have no idea if that is going to be enough for you or not).

◆ † ◆

♦ CHAPTER THIRTEEN ♦

CHOOSING A FINANCIAL ADVISOR

Financial advising is just like every other profession. You have your great advisors, your awful advisors, and most fall somewhere in-between… There are some really smart advisors who consistently have their client's best interest in mind as they help them achieve financial success. I love that there are advisors out there doing this good work. However, while many advisors have good intentions; they may lack a sufficient knowledge of the industry to consistently provide good advice. No matter how much regulation is imposed on the profession (and there is a lot!), there are always going to be some advisors who just aren't very good at their jobs. In addition, a very few are just flat out unscrupulous…

If you can find a good advisor, then you are set. But here is the thing; it's hard to know… I think about Bernie Madoff. He had a great reputation and experience in the industry that was unrivaled – but he was a complete crook! He conned hundreds of people out of their hard-earned dollars in his infamous Ponzi scheme. While I have no evidence to back this up, I would bet that Kevin Bacon (a client of Madoff and one of my all-time favorite actors) thought Bernie was a super nice guy and a great financial advisor until he saw on the news that Madoff was being trotted off to prison for securities fraud.

This may sound strange, but the skill-set that makes most advisors successful isn't their ability to consistently provide good advice. What makes an advisor successful is their "people-ability". You could be the smartest advisor in the world – but if you are unprofessional and somewhat unlikable, you probably won't be successful in the profession. Because advisors are generally good with people, it's sometimes difficult to recognize if they are helping you or really just helping themselves.

Another issue that may make finding a good advisor difficult for you is the fact that many of them may not want you as their client. Not to sound harsh, but it is possible that many advisors will not want to work with you. Many successful advisors try to avoid (and even cull out) all but the highest net worth clients. Based on the way that many advisors are paid; they earn the bulk of their compensation from the assets they hold under their management. If you don't have much in the way of assets yet, they won't make very much; therefore, they aren't very motivated to have you as a client...

Finding a financial advisor you like (and wants you as a client) may prove difficult. However, there are plenty of great ones out there; and to help you find them, I'm going to go over three primary criteria that I think are important considerations. These criteria are the financial advisor's compensation method, experience, and education. However, before I do that, let me direct you to a few slightly user-unfriendly but really helpful websites, www.investmentadvisorsearch.org is one particularly helpful website and www.adviserinfo.sec.gov is another. On these two websites, you will be able to search out and find all the information that is publicly available on an advisor. In particular, you will be able to peruse the advisor's Form ADV. This isn't the most user-friendly form either, but it does have a wealth of information on it if you want to do some serious research on your advisor.

Compensation

While I'm sure there are some great advisors with other types of compensation methods, it is my opinion that it makes sense to try to find what is known as a "fee-only" financial planner. In fact, I think the financial planning industry is moving entirely toward a "fee-only" platform because of its natural attributes. Don't get this confused with a "fee-based" financial planner. This type of advisor is still popular but has an entirely different compensation method from a "fee-only" planner. Fee-only planners will blatantly state "fee-only" on their marketing materials and website. They will likely be proud of this compensation method and want to make it known. In fact, some advisors may even advertise "fee-only" when in fact, they are not. So be sure to do your research and understand how the advisor is paid.

A "fee-only" advisor will charge you a flat fee upfront before doing any work for you. A good advisor will tell you exactly what they will do and how much it will cost. The advisor should give you a document known as a "brochure" before contracting any business with you. Don't just throw it away! It is required to be written in a way that you can easily understand, and contains a wealth of useful information on the advisor's business.

In the initial meeting (which should always be complimentary), the advisor should ask you many questions about your financial life. They do this (in part) to help them determine the complexity of your case, and the amount of work they are going to have to do for you. This will impact the level of the fee (more complex cases will typically have a higher associated fee). The amount of the fee is entirely up to the advisor, and the decision to pay it is entirely up to you. The important thing to keep in mind is the fact that you can always walk away if you don't like the deal you are getting.

If you choose to work with a "fee-only" planner, after they provide you with the financial planning service that you acquired for the upfront fee, they may also offer you the opportunity to place your investment assets with them. This likely means that they will provide you with (or help you set up) a brokerage account and manage your investments. This decision is also entirely up to you. If you choose to let the fee-only advisor invest your assets for you, they will likely charge you a percentage each year on the value of the account. This charge is typically between 0.5% and 2.5% of the account's value and many advisors base this fee on the amount invested (large amounts get a better rate). While I'm not a fan of paying any more fees than I have to pay, this fee may not be a totally bad thing. The more they are able to make for you – the more they make. In addition, if they are making consistent money from you, they are likely going to be motivated to keep you as a client, and thus, make every effort to keep you happy… That being said, I still contend that lower fees are better…

I equate using the fee-only planner to manage your investments to eating out at a restaurant. You could make the meal at home yourself. There is nothing stopping you. However, even though you can do it at home for a lower expense, you might still choose to eat out, and let someone else worry about the buying, cooking, presenting and cleaning up after the meal. In addition, it is possible that the chef at the restaurant is just simply a better cook than you. But just like the restaurant, the fee-only planner is going to try to make a profit. It's their job.

Commission-based or fee-based financial planners may seem like they have lower fees to start than the fee-only planner, but keep in mind that commissions are paid every time you make a trade or purchase certain types of products (like annuities and insurance). These commissions may provide advisors with an inherent conflict of interest which may compensate the advisor for making recommendations that are not in your best interest.

In summary, I know there are some great fee-and-commission based advisors out there. There are also likely some terrible fee-only advisors. However, since there is really no way for me to tell you how to separate the good from the bad, choosing a fee-only planner at least filters out some of the opportunity for the advisor to take advantage of you.

Experience

Experience counts. I felt like I was a fantastic financial advisor my first day on the job. I didn't want to do anything except help people. How can you go wrong with those pure motives? Now, in hindsight, I was just too ignorant of the industry to truly be able to help many people early in my career. I knew what my firm wanted me to know. Looking back now, I agree with most of it, but I disagree with a lot of the strategies they suggested for me to pursue with my clients. The fact is that at the time, I just didn't have the necessary experience to be discerning of good information and strategies. I have some regrets…

You may be approached by your peers (fellow recent graduates) who have decided to pursue financial advising as their career. I'm not exactly going to advise you against hiring them, but I think you need to be careful. First off – brand new advisors are not only willing to take you on as a client; they would be absolutely thrilled to be your advisor. Enthusiasm can go a long way, but they still need experience. If you are going to work with an advisor with less than three years' experience, I suggest that you be sure that they have a mentor or another experienced advisor working closely with them.

Another warning about new advisors is that there tends to be a lot of turnover in the profession. Be prepared to have your new advisor quit. Your account will likely then be turned over to another "struggling" advisor within the firm. This could work out fine, but then again…

Education

Let me state right off the bat my personal bias when it comes to education. I'm going to suggest that your advisor has a Certified Financial Planner™ (CFP®) certification. I'm obviously biased here, because I have one. The CFP certification is not the "end-all, be-all" when it comes to finding a good financial advisor. There are some great advisors out there without any designations. However, it does suggest that your advisor has met some pretty high education and experience standards. In addition, those with the CFP designation have stated that they promise to act in accordance with the high ethical standards set by the Certified Financial Planner Board of Standards. You can actually search www.cfp.net to find CFP professionals in your area. The website will also tell you if the advisor is "fee-only" …

NOTE: *Other impressive certifications include the Chartered Financial Analyst (CFA) and the Certified Public Accountant (CPA). These designations have required a serious commitment on the part of the holder. While impressive, in my experience, the CFA and CPA are not as popular among financial advisors as the CFP.*

Other than the CFP, there are dozens of other letters that your advisor may advertise after his or her name. Most of the time, these designations do signify a certain dedication to the profession. But don't just see some letters and assume the advisor is educated in your financial planning area. I suggest that you type the letters into an Internet search, and read up on what they mean and the requirements to obtain them. You may be surprised.

Investing on-line

Whether or not you choose to utilize a fee-only financial advisor, you will still have the option to implement his or her advice yourself by investing on-line. This is like having your meals at home instead of eating at a restaurant. Restaurants are nice, but you may be able to prepare some tasty meals yourself with less cost than eating out.

If you run an Internet search on "investing on-line" you are likely to be overwhelmed by your options. Unfortunately, I don't think any single brokerage is going to be best for everyone. You are going to need to do some research on your own to find the on-line brokerage site that you like best. Some of the popular on-line investing options include: E-Trade, Scottrade, TD Ameritrade, Fidelity, Charles Schwab, and Vanguard. Before choosing, be sure to explore the site of the different brokerages. Many of them have a wealth of information about different investments and investing strategies. The help they provide may assist you in choosing the right brokerage for you.

NOTE: *I believe almost without exception, you will need a bank account before you will be able to invest on-line. However, many of these brokerages also offer banking products like savings accounts if you want to have your entire financial life under one roof.*

       I am not currently (and have no plans to become) compensated by the six brokerage sites I listed (or any others).

Opening up your account

I believe if you visit any of the homepages for any of the companies I just mentioned, you will find a button that states "Open an Account" in a bright color and big bold letters. These firms want to make it easy for you to find what you need. They want your business!

To finish setting up the account, the brokerage is going to ask you for the following information (these steps could take place in any order):

- You are going to be asked what kind of an account you would like. Do you want a "single" account that is just for you or a "joint" account for you and your spouse? Do you want a "brokerage" account which is a taxable account or do you want a "Roth IRA" or "Traditional IRA"?

- Once you select the type of account you want to open, then you will be asked how much money you want to invest and in what investment (remember – in chapter eleven, I suggested a money market fund to open the account). Many brokerages may require at least $1,000 or even more before allowing you to open an account. *NOTE: You will be asked if you want to reinvest the dividends/interest/income… If you want the power of compound growth – the answer is always "Yes".*

- At some point, you are going to need to tell them your name, address, phone number, etc. You may even be asked some fairly personal questions about your net worth and income. There is a good reason they are asking for this (regulations), so be sure to answer truthfully…

- You will need to provide a Social Security number. If you do not have one, you will need to contact a representative from the broker to determine if you have any other options.

- You will also be asked for your email address and your preferences for receiving information on your investments (mail or email). *NOTE: You may be able to avoid some service fees if you agree to have documents delivered electronically.*

- Sooner or later, they will want you to create a user name and password that will allow you to log-in and check the status of your accounts at any point going forward.

- To seal the deal, you will be asked how you want to send the money to open the account. Two popular choices are to have the money sent electronically from your bank (in which case you will need your bank information handy) or you can mail them a check.

That's really about it... Pretty easy stuff in the realm of it all...

◆ † ◆

♦ EPILOGUE ♦

THE MEANING OF SUCCESS

This book has attempted to provide you with some of the tools you will need to achieve "financial success" but what does success look like for you? Success for one person might be to afford an apartment in a nicer neighborhood. Success for another person might be to afford a new car. A third person might define success by achieving the financial independence needed to retire early. How do you define financial success for you?

What needs are you trying to meet?

To aid you in defining what "financial success" means for you, it may be helpful to think about what needs you are trying to meet. If you have ever taken a psychology class, you may remember Abraham Maslow's hierarchy of needs. Maslow stated that people are motivated to achieve certain needs and that some needs take precedence over others. For instance, if you don't have your basic "physiological" needs met (food, water, warmth, rest), then you are probably more motivated to meet these needs than anything else. However, once your physiological needs have been met, then you are likely to progress to the next level of needs, and so on.

Maslow's hierarchy consists of the following five levels of needs:

1. *Physiological* – the most basic of all human needs (food, water, sustenance)
2. *Safety* – the need for security, protection and stability in day-to-day life
3. *Social* – the need for affection, friendships, and belongingness with other people
4. *Esteem* – the need for respect, prestige, recognition of competency or mastery
5. *Self-actualization* – the highest level of need fulfillment that includes growth and achieving one's fullest potential (finding meaning in life)

Which needs are you currently trying to meet from a financial standpoint? If you are just struggling to pay your bills, then you may be trying to meet your physiological financial needs. If you are uncomfortable with the security of your current apartment and would like to afford a nicer home, according to Maslow, your finances are likely dedicated to meeting your safety needs. What if you are trying to save up for a nice new car? Then you may be trying to meet esteem needs.

Interestingly, even our most important long-term financial goals typically fall under Maslow's lower-order needs. For instance, "having enough money in retirement", while terribly important, is really just meeting a safety need. In fact, you can likely achieve "financial success" without ever reaching Maslow's highest-order need of self-actualization. Can you think of anything else you might be able to do with your money that may help you grow and achieve your fullest potential – to self-actualize? From a strictly financial standpoint, perhaps the easiest way to begin to meet your self-actualization needs is to simply give to others.

Giving back – really?

It is entirely possible that this may not be the time for you to attempt to self-actualize. If you are attempting to meet other lower-order needs, then you may want to achieve these financial successes first. In addition, I truly understand how frustrated you might be at the idea of giving back, considering the difficulty that you are likely to have in meeting your own needs. Making matters worse is the fact that society is really taking a lot from you and seemingly has no intention of giving you back nearly as much as it takes. As I stated in the prologue, it is my personal belief that you will be taxed heavily to help others, but no one is going to help you. The deck is stacked against you! And you MUST take care of yourselves over your lifetime by making smart financial choices today.

But think about this a moment: how many stories have you heard about people who had the deck stacked against them – but didn't let that stop them? They worked to achieve greatness despite adversity.

- **Abraham Lincoln** – was born into a very poor family, had to educate himself, but eventually became President of the United States

- **Nelson Mandela** – went to prison for almost thirty years before being released and working to

163

end apartheid and becoming the first black President of South Africa

- **Helen Keller** – was born blind and deaf, but became the first deaf/blind person to obtain a Bachelor of Arts degree and later became a world-famous author and lecturer

- **Moses** – was targeted for death as an infant and spent many years in exile for killing a man before leading a people out of slavery and becoming the most important prophet in Judaism

- **J.K. Rowling** – while struggling on welfare to support her daughter, considered suicide before becoming tremendously successful for creating the "Harry Potter" books

- **Malala Yousafzai** – survived an assassination attempt at the age of fifteen before becoming one of the world's most popular activists against the Taliban's prohibition on the education of girls

- **Albert Einstein** – was targeted by the Nazis before becoming the world's most influential physicist

Do you have it much worse than any of these people?

And I'm just spouting off some stories from the top of my head… I'm sure you know others. We know the stories of these people because they have been tremendous successes! They are "heroes". We admire them and in some cases, strive to be like them! Here is your chance!

Making the list

Society is going to take and take from you. How about giving even more? It sounds crazy, given my potential understanding of your financial predicament, that I'd suggest that you also "give back". But that is exactly what I'm going to do. These taxes you pay to assist others are an obligation. You have to pay them and it probably doesn't feel very good at all. Giving is not an obligation. Giving is something entirely different and that difference is powerful.

There are a lot of great lessons that can be learned from the Sermon on the Mount. However, I only want to focus on a few verses that Jesus teaches in chapter five of the Book of Matthew:

> *[41] If someone forces you to go one mile, go with him two miles. [42] Give to the one who asks you, and do not turn away from the one who wants to borrow from you.*

For many years, I read these verses and thought that Jesus was trying to teach me to do more for people than I had to. Not a bad lesson in and of itself... But a while back, I found out additional background on this particular parable. David Guzik on www.enduringword.com writes of verse 41.

> *Positively, we are told to take command of evil impositions by making a deliberate choice to give more than we are required. At that time, Judea was under Roman military occupation. Under military law, any Roman soldier might command a Jew to carry his soldier's pack for one mile - but only one mile. Jesus here says, "go beyond the one mile*

165

*required by law and give another mile out of a free
choice of love." This is how we transform an attempt
to manipulate us into a free act of love.*

Being financially-minded, I immediately related this to
the difference between taxes (the first mile) and gifts (the
second mile). For years, I'd complained and griped about
all the taxes I had to pay. Giving was not important to
me. "I give all the time – I work and pay taxes!" But I
wasn't giving. I was meeting an obligation and this verse
helped me understand that there is a difference. When I
understood Jesus' true meaning of this verse – I decided
to try to make a change. In trying to implement this in my
own life, I've noticed a huge difference in my day-to-day
perceptions. From a financial standpoint, I'm at least
trying to meet some sort of self-actualization need and the
impact of this effort has actually made me more content.
If I'm being completely honest, "giving" is not a behavior
that comes very naturally to me, but the more I work on
it, the happier I get. Who couldn't benefit from additional
happiness?

Just like any other financial goal, you can budget for your
giving. And just like any other financial goal, you may
not be able to budget as much as you would like. To go
back to the parable for a moment, if for you the extra
"mile" is only a foot or two – then better to go the extra
foot than not. It is still a self-actualizing behavior if you
give what you can. If you make a concerted effort to give
"something" today, then I'm confident that over time the
good feelings you enjoy from that giving will only cause
you to establish the goal of giving more when you can. In
fact, if you can't come up with any financial gifts today,
then you can still give of your time. Sometimes this can
make even more of a difference than money! And it will
still have the same positive impact on your psyche.

In closing, imagine this being true of you... You have the odds stacked against you, but you don't succumb to them. You achieve success despite the odds! And all the while, you are giving back to society more than it asks of you. That's the kind of person I'd put on my hero list.

Good luck and God bless...

♦ ♦ † ♦ ♦

END NOTES

Prologue

Covey, S. R. (2013). *The 7 habits of highly effective people: Powerful lessons in personal change.* Simon & Schuster.

Wucker, M. (2016). *The gray rhino: How to recognize and act on the obvious dangers we ignore.* St. Martin's Press.

Chapter Two

Hill, N. (2008). *Think and grow rich.* Wilder.

Kiyosaki, R. T. (2011). *Rich dad poor dad: What the rich teach their kids about money that the poor and middle class do not!* Plata.

Carnegie, D. (1998). *How to win friends & influence people.* Pocket Books.

Fisher, R. & Ury, W. (2011). *Getting to yes: Negotiating agreement without giving in.* Penguin Books.

Chapter Three

Howard, C. (2013). *Clark Howard's living large for the long haul: Consumer-tested ways to overhaul your finances, increase your savings, and get your life back on track.* Avery.

Howard, C. (2011). *Clark Howard's living large in lean times: 250+ ways to buy smarter, spend smarter, and save money.* Avery.

Chapter Eleven

Malkiel, B. G. (2016). *A random walk down Wall Street: The time-tested strategy of successful investing.* W. W. Norton & Co.

Cramer, J. J. (2013). *Jim Cramer's Get rich carefully.* Blue Rider Press.

GLOSSARY

457 – retirement plan primarily for government employees

401(k) – retirement plan primarily for businesses

403(b) – retirement plan primarily for nonprofits

Actively-managed fund – fund manager attempts to beat the market

Adjusted gross income – income minus specific reductions

Adjustable rate mortgage – variable rate mortgage

Baby boomers – generation born between 1946 & 1964

Balance sheet – snapshot of assets & liabilities

Balanced fund – fund that invests in stocks & bonds

Balloon mortgage – mortgage with balance due in short term

Bankruptcy – legal declaration of inability to pay creditors

Beneficiary – recipient of benefits

Bond – debt security

Brochure – written disclosure of an investment advisor

Brokerage – financial firm that buys & sells securities for clients

Budget – inflows minus outflows

Business plan – document that describes a new business's concepts and goals

Capital gain – sales price is higher than purchase price

Cashier's check – check backed by a financial institution

Certificate of deposit (CD) – interest-bearing promissory note from a bank

Check cashing service – firm that cashes a check for a fee

Commercial bank – financial firm that provides traditional banking services

Commission – broker charge for handling financial transactions

Common stock – security representing company ownership

Compound return – reinvested earning's growth on growth

Conventional mortgage – level payment mortgage for fixed term

Corporate bond – debt security of a company

Credit card – allows owner to borrow funds for purchases

Credit rating agency – company that evaluates debtor's ability to pay off debt

Credit score – indication to lender of borrower's ability to pay off debt

Credit union – member owned institution that offers traditional banking services

Death benefit – proceeds of a life insurance policy

Debit card – bank card allowing for the electronic transfer of money

Deductible – amount payable before insurance benefits are paid

Deduction – amount subtracted from gross income reducing tax due

Defined benefit plan – retirement benefits paid to an employee by an employer

Defined contribution plan – retirement plan with contributions made by employee and sometimes employer

Disability insurance – benefits paid when insured cannot work

Discretionary income – amount remaining after savings & expenses

Diversification – reducing risk by investing in many different assets

Dividend – company profits paid to shareholders

Dollar cost averaging – regular fixed investment savings

Down payment – amount due up front at onset of purchase

Draft account – credit union checking account

Earned income – taxable pay received for work

Emergency fund – savings set aside for emergencies

Exchange traded fund – security that tracks an index

FDIC – government corporation insuring bank deposits

Federal income tax – charge imposed on earnings

Fee-based advisor – financial advisor who charges a percentage of assets and/or commissions

Fee-only advisor – financial advisor who charges a fee for advice and/or a percentage of assets

FICA tax – deductions from income to pay Social Security & Medicare benefits

Financial asset – asset without management responsibility

Flat tax – same tax is paid by everyone

Franchise –business that licenses use of business model

Fraud protection – protects consumers from fraudulent activity

FUTA – unemployment tax paid by employers

Government bond – debt security of a government

Grace period – period in which payment can be made without fees

Graduated mortgage – mortgage with increasing payments

HDHP – high deductible health plan

Health insurance – covers risk of medical expenses

HMO – health maintenance organization

HSA – health savings account

Interest – amount paid for borrowed money

Intermediate-term bond – debt security with 3-10 year maturity

Internship – a position in a firm designed for a student to gain experience

Investment benchmark – standard in which an investment is compared to assess performance

Investment – asset purchased with the goal of increased value

Itemized deduction – certain expenses that decrease taxable income

Large-cap – large U.S. companies

Lease (auto) – renting for a specific period

Life insurance – benefits paid to beneficiary when insured dies

Load fund – fund with a sales charge

Long-term bond – debt security with over 10 year maturity

Long-term care insurance – benefits paid when insured requires assistance with daily activities

Marginal tax – tax due on next dollar of income

Market capitalization – total dollar market value of company's shares

Medicaid – health services for low-income

Medicare – social health insurance for age 65 and older

Mid-cap – mid-size U.S. companies

Minimum balance – amount that must be kept in an account

Minimum payment – smallest allowable payment on a credit card

Money laundering – schemes to make illegally obtained money appear legal

Money market account – FDIC insured fund that invests in short-term debt securities

Money market fund – non FDIC insured fund that invests in short-term debt securities

Mortgage (home) – loan for the purpose of buying a house

Mutual fund family – group of mutual funds offered by one investment company

Mutual fund – a basket of securities purchased from the pooled funds of investors

NCUSIF – federal fund insuring credit unions

Network – a group of developed contacts with other people

Net worth – assets minus liabilities

No load fund – fund without a sales charge

Overdraft protection – credit line banks offer to protect customers from writing checks over account value

Passively- managed fund – fund manager attempts to obtain market return

Pension plan – retirement plan where employer makes contributions for employee benefit

Permanent life insurance – cash value insurance designed to stay in-force until death

PITI – principal, interest, taxes, insurance

PMI – private mortgage insurance

PPO – preferred provider organization

Portfolio – combination of investments

Prepaid card – preloaded card with a set amount of dollars

Principal – [1] amount borrowed or still owed on loan [2] original investment

Progressive tax – tax that increases with income

Rate of return – gain/loss on an investment over specified period

Real asset – asset with management responsibility

Real estate agent – represents buyer or seller in real estate transaction

Required minimum distribution – specified amount that must be distributed from a qualified plan at a certain age

Roth IRA – individual retirement account with unique tax treatment

S&P 500 – large-cap stock market index

Secured card – card backed by savings account

SEP – retirement plan primarily used by small business

Share account – credit union savings account

Short-term bond- debt security with less than 2 years until maturity

SIMPLE – retirement plan primarily used by small business

Small-cap – small size U.S. companies

Social Security – benefits paid to retirees, unemployed and disabled

Standard deduction – amount subtracted from taxable income without itemization

Subsidized loan – government pays for interest on loan while student is in school

Tax credit – sum that can offset taxes owed

Taxable income – amount used to calculate tax due

Term insurance – life insurance designed to remain in-force for a specific period

Time value of money – money now is worth more than in the future due to its earning capacity

Total income – sum of all money received

Traditional IRA – individual retirement account with tax deductible/deferred treatment

Unsubsidized loan – interest begins accruing as soon as loan is taken

Vesting – process of earning the right to receive benefits

Withholding – funds withheld from regular pay to help meet tax liability

ABOUT THE AUTHOR

C. Michael Smith began working in 1999 as a Financial Advisor and later as a Financial Planning Analyst for a large investment company in Roanoke, Virginia. In 2001, he became the Director of Plan Design at a boutique investments and insurance firm in Richmond, Virginia. During this time, he obtained the Series 7, 66, and 24 licenses, as well as the Chartered Financial Consultant (ChFC) and the Certified Financial Planner (CFP) certifications. In 2003, he returned to academia to pursue his Ph.D. in Resource Management, which he completed in 2007. His dissertation topic was on the information-seeking efforts of investors.

Dr. Smith developed a passion for helping young people make smart financial choices as a graduate student working with undergraduates. He is still active in these efforts today as a lecturer at a small private college in Virginia, teaching courses in risk management, personal finance, and investments. He has also written an introductory textbook for undergraduates, *Investments: Fundamental Theory & Practice*, published by Textbook Media Press.

www.ingramcontent.com/pod-product-compliance
Lightning Source LLC
Chambersburg PA
CBHW031957190326
41520CB00007B/276

* 9 780099 478225 *